The
CBT
Workbook
— for —

Anxious Teens

57 Exercises to Find Relief from
Worry, Panic, Negative Thinking & Perfectionism

Angela M. Doel, MS, and **Lawrence E. Shapiro**, PhD

PESI Publishing
pesipublishing.com

About the Authors

Angela M. Doel, MS, is a writer and director of operations at Between Sessions Resources. She has served in various clinical supervisory positions and worked as a family therapist. Ms. Doel earned her MS in Counseling Psychology at the University of Pennsylvania. She holds an advanced certificate in nutritional counseling, and her areas of specialization are health education and eating disorders.

Lawrence E. Shapiro, PhD, is a prolific author of self-help books and the inventor of more than 100 therapeutic games. Dr. Shapiro is known for his practical approach to helping others. He has written workbooks, storybooks, card games, board games, and smartphone apps. His work has been translated into 27 languages.

Table of Contents

Introduction vii

section 1

Understand Your Anxiety 1

Is Anxiety a Problem for You? 2

Will Your Worries Actually Come True? 5

Does Your Worrying Make You Sick? 9

Does Your Anxiety Affect the People Around You? 12

Understand Social Anxiety 15

How Distressed Are You in Social Situations? 17

Understand and Track Your Panic Attacks 20

Are You Oversensitive to Criticism? 24

Are You Afraid to Be Away from Your Parents or Caregivers? 27

Do You Have Health Anxiety? 30

How Do Avoidance Behaviors Impact Your Life? 32

Are You Too Rigid About Routines and Schedules? 35

Do You Have Depression Along with Anxiety? 37

section 2

How Anxiety Affects Your Social and Academic Life—and What to Do About It! 43

Identify Your Worst Fears About Social Situations 44

Are You Avoiding School? 47

How to Handle School Pressure 50

Do You Worry About Your Grades? 54

Feel Less Anxious When Taking Tests 56

Feel Less Anxious During School Presentations 59

Missing Out Because You're Anxious 63

Understand How Social Media Affects Your Social Anxiety 66

Reduce Your Self-Consciousness in Social Situations 70

There's Nothing Small About Small Talk 73

Are You Anxious About Going on Dates? 75

Exposure Therapy for Dating Anxiety 77

section 3	**More Techniques to Overcome Anxiety**	**81**

Using a Worry Log 82

Using Humor to Stop Worrying 85

Using a Worry Script 88

Alter Your Symmetry Rituals 90

Reduce All-or-Nothing Thinking 94

Talk Back to the Thoughts That Make You Anxious 96

How Do You View Yourself? 100

It's Okay if You're Not Perfect! 105

Face Your Fears with Acceptance and Commitment Therapy 109

What to Do When You Worry Too Much About Your Health 112

Using Visual Metaphors to Accept Your Worries and Distressing Thoughts 115

Controlling Your Hair Pulling 119

Stop Yourself from Fainting When You Get a Shot or Have Blood Drawn 122

Curb Your Compulsions to Diminish Your Anxiety 125

Reduce Overstimulation to Focus on Yourself 128

Mindful Meditation 101 132

Become Mindful of Your World Rather Than Your Anxious Thoughts 135

section 4	**Change Your Thinking**	**139**

Own Your Thoughts 140

Become Aware of the Physical Reactions to Your Distressing Thoughts 142

Confront Thoughts That Make You Anxious 146

Five Steps to Deal with Intrusive Thoughts 149

Your Mind Is Playing Tricks on You 152

You Don't Need Constant Reassurance 156

Tolerate and Overcome Physical Discomfort 159

Anticipate Success 163

Fill Your Mind with Positive Thoughts 165

section 5	**Lifestyle Changes**	**169**

Changing Your Diet to Help Your Anxiety 170

Mindfulness—Just This Breath 174

Stretch Out of Your Comfort Zone 175

Exercise to Overcome Anxiety 179

Sleeping Better to Reduce Anxiety 181

Prevent and Manage Lapses in Overcoming Your Anxiety 184

Introduction

Fear and worry are commonly experienced by adolescents as a normal part of growing up. But when these emotions get in the way of a teen's daily life and disrupt their routine, this could be a sign of an anxiety disorder.

When Is Anxiety a Problem for an Adolescent?

Although everyone experiences anxiety, some teens begin to feel anxious and/or worried so often or so intensely that it makes them feel uncomfortable and begins to interfere with their daily lives. This might show up as an extreme response to a situation or event they believe is threatening, and the intensity of the reaction might be out of proportion to the actual danger. This response often includes worrying about harm or danger, heightened physical responses, and the avoidance of situations, places, or events—leading to considerable distress that interferes with their daily activities at school, at home, or with friends.

Other common ways in which teens may experience anxiety include:

- Panic attacks
- Obsessions and/or compulsions
- Perfectionism
- Selective mutism, in which a teen does not speak in certain situations
- Anxiety when separated from a parent or caregiver
- Avoidance of social situations
- Excessive worrying

Anxiety affects 32 percent of American adolescents ages 13 to 18.[1] Over the past 20 years, the number of anxious teens has been steadily increasing. And 80 percent of kids with diagnosable anxiety disorders fail to receive appropriate treatment—though anxiety disorders are highly treatable.[2]

Research shows that treatment of mild anxiety should begin with therapy. However, if the teen suffers from moderate to severe anxiety, a combination of medication and therapy might be the best approach. Cognitive behavioral therapy (CBT) is an effective and appropriate treatment for adolescents with anxiety disorders. The worksheets in this book are intended to be used as tools to complement the therapeutic approaches you use with your adolescent clients. They are designed to increase clients' awareness of the relationships between their emotions, thoughts, physical sensations, and anxiety. The assignments provide steps for clients to manage their distress and anxious thoughts in healthier ways.

---

[1] National Institute of Mental Health. (2017, November). *Any anxiety disorder.* https://www.nimh.nih.gov/health/statistics/any-anxiety-disorder

[2] Anxiety and Depression Association of America. (n.d.). *Children and teens.* https://adaa.org/find-help/by-demographics/children/children-teens

It Is Time for Teens to Overcome Their Anxiety

There are many factors that contribute to the increase in anxiety disorders in teens. In addition to genetics, brain chemistry, personality, and life events, consider the following factors:

- Increasingly high expectations and pressure to succeed
- Living in a world that feels scary and threatening
- Pressure from friends to use substances like alcohol or recreational drugs
- Constant connection via electronic devices to social media and messaging apps

Whatever the cause, this rise in anxiety is a real problem for teens.

Chronic anxiety may lead to serious mental health problems: depression, substance abuse, and even suicide. Anxiety interferes with teens' ability to focus and learn, leading to academic problems that can have lifelong impacts. Teens may also experience physical problems, such as headaches, chronic pain, or digestive problems.

The CBT Workbook for Anxious Teens was written to help teens manage and reduce the sometimes debilitating symptoms of anxiety. The assignments can be thought of as therapy homework, and you can explain to your adolescent clients why each exercise is important, guiding them in learning new emotional, cognitive, and behavioral skills that can reduce their anxiety.

This workbook offers dozens of worksheets that will help teens learn strategies to manage their anxiety in constructive ways, instead of turning to unhealthy or harmful coping strategies. Each worksheet is written specifically for adolescent clients in a manner that is practical, user-friendly, and easy to understand. While no single worksheet is effective for everyone, we are confident you will discover techniques that inspire change.

The Importance of Therapeutic Homework

For new skills to be most effective, your clients need to practice them regularly between counseling sessions. Using homework assignments, teens can rehearse new coping strategies to effectively manage anxiety, strengthening the insights and intentions that surface during counseling sessions.

Research suggests that homework enhances the effectiveness of counseling sessions, and clients who complete homework assignments on a consistent basis tend to have better outcomes. In addition to giving the counseling context and focus, homework provides concrete feedback for the counselor about a client's progress. For instance, when there are issues with homework compliance, counselors can identify obstacles and challenges to the client's goal achievement.

How to Use This Workbook

Each worksheet has three sections: Objective, What to Know, and What to Do. The **Objective** states what the client should expect to have accomplished upon completion of the worksheet. The **What to Know** section offers background information about the issue(s) being addressed in the worksheet. Finally, the

What to Do component features a variety of exercises or tools, including thought-provoking questions to answer, charts to track activities, and questionnaires to complete.

You can recommend or purchase this book for your adolescent clients, and they can write directly on the pages and bring it to each counseling session for further discussion. You can also pick and choose the most appropriate worksheets, print them off or email them, and assign them to your clients each week. Regardless of how you use this workbook, you will certainly find worksheets that are helpful for your anxious teen clients.

Understand
Your
Anxiety

section 1

worksheet

Is Anxiety a Problem for You?

Objective

To identify the symptoms of anxiety and determine if those symptoms are creating problems in your life.

What to Know

Everyone experiences anxiety, and sometimes worry or fearfulness signals danger, letting you know that you need to leave a situation or be on high alert. However, sometimes anxiety becomes exaggerated and unhealthy, limiting your experiences and impacting your social life, relationships, and how well you function at home and in school.

Teens deal with lots of changes and uncertainties. But, for some teens, anxiety becomes a chronic state that interferes with their ability to live and perform at their highest potential. Participating in extracurricular and social activities, as well as making and keeping friends, become challenging.

Sometimes anxiety is a generalized, free-floating feeling of unease or worry, or it develops into panic attacks or phobias. Do you know the common symptoms of anxiety? They are:

- Excessive fear and worry
- Restlessness
- Wariness or uneasiness
- Constant nervousness
- Heightened self-consciousness
- Being overly shy or introverted
- Frequent thoughts of losing control
- Unrealistic concerns about social or academic competence
- Intense fear of a specific object or activity
- Obsessions (repeating thoughts) or compulsions (repeating actions to relieve anxiety)

You might also have physical symptoms, such as sensations of unreality, shortness of breath, headaches, trembling, sweating, muscle tension, choking sensations, chest pains, stomachaches, nausea, dizziness, and numbness or tingling in the arms or legs.

What to Do

The following list includes some common thoughts, feelings, physical sensations, and behaviors that people have when they are anxious. Check off the statements that apply to you. If there are other anxiety-related thoughts, feelings, physical sensations, or behaviors you have that are missing from the list, add them at the end.

_____ People tell me I worry a lot.

_____ I have a hard time controlling and changing my thoughts.

_____ I get annoyed and snap at people when I'm anxious.

_____ There are events or experiences from my past that trigger anxious feelings.

_____ If I have an upcoming event (for example, a big test or class presentation), I worry about it for days or weeks.

_____ I feel on edge, like I'm waiting for something bad to happen.

_____ I get upset when things don't go my way or plans change.

_____ I worry about what people are thinking or saying about me.

_____ I have a hard time focusing or paying attention because I'm distracted by worry.

_____ I think about the same things over and over again.

_____ I feel like I'm going crazy or losing my mind.

_____ I take even small things really seriously.

_____ When I'm really anxious I sweat, shake, feel light-headed, or experience other unpleasant body sensations.

_____ I avoid certain places or things because they make me anxious.

_____ There are activities or behaviors that I do over and over again.

_____ My mind races and I have a hard time falling asleep.

_____ I spend time thinking about things I can't control or worrying about what might happen in the future.

_____ I avoid talking with people I don't know.

_____ I'm afraid I will embarrass or humiliate myself.

_____ I usually focus on what can go wrong.

_____ Worrying makes me feel sick.

_____ I avoid going to dances, to parties, or out on dates.

_____ There is too much pressure to get good grades.

_____ I get really nervous taking tests or presenting in class.

_____ I don't like to try new things.

_____ I use drugs or alcohol to deal with my anxiety.

_____ I am afraid of something specific (for example, dogs, thunderstorms, the dark, riding in an airplane, receiving an injection, being away from my parents or caregivers): _____

_____ Other: _____

_____ Other: _____

_____ Other: _____

Add up your number of checks. How many did you check off? _____

If you checked off more than ten statements, anxiety may be a problem for you.

What areas of your life have been negatively affected by your anxiety?

_____

_____

_____

What do you do to deal with anxiety?

_____

_____

_____

Name someone you can talk to about this problem: _____

worksheet

Will Your Worries Come True?

Objective

To understand and accept that events are influenced by the laws of probability rather than your worries.

What to Know

When you worry, you focus on what you think might happen in the future. You might imagine all the ways the situation could turn out—especially the ways it could turn out badly. Your worries might revolve around situations you can't control, and you might believe that something terrible will happen if you don't act in a certain way. While feeling overwhelmed, you might not realistically examine whether what you fear most is likely to come true. Just because something is possible doesn't mean it's probable. Anxiety can make it difficult to distinguish between what's possible and what's probable.

Consider Ryan, a 16-year-old high school junior. He earns good grades and is involved in lots of activities. He has many friends, and he gets along with his brother and sister. Unfortunately, Ryan spends hours worrying and preparing for the upcoming SAT (Scholastic Aptitude Test) that is required for college admissions. He worries about doing terribly on the test, disappointing his parents, and failing to get admitted into college. Ryan is losing sleep and struggling to get through the day. The test is three months away.

What if Ryan applied the theory of probability to his worries? Probability is the likelihood that an event will occur. Is it likely that if Ryan prepares for the test, he will do poorly? Of course, it's always possible that his fear is warranted, but is it probable? Many teens with anxiety imagine the worst outcome and act accordingly to prevent it. But think about this: If it's possible for the worst outcome to occur, it's also possible for the best outcome to take place. Ryan's life is negatively impacted by his anxiety over doing well on a test.

What to Do

This worksheet will help your rational mind better understand the concept of probability. Begin by thinking about something you worry about because you think it could have a terrible outcome. Then you will look at nine other possible outcomes. With each outcome, you'll consider the likelihood (probability) that the outcome will happen and why.

First, review the example. Then, fill in the blank chart. In the first row, write down the worst outcome you can imagine. In the remaining rows, write down nine other possible outcomes, making sure that at least three of the possibilities are positive ones.

Finally, go back and write in the probability that each outcome will occur (low, medium, or high) and the reasons for your probability estimate.

Possible Outcome	Probability	Reasons/Comments
I'll be so nervous during my class presentation that I'll faint, and my classmates will make fun of me.	Low	I'll eat a snack before class and practice my deep breathing so I know I won't faint. And my classmates aren't that mean—if I did faint, they'd help me, not make fun of me.
I'll spill a glass of water during the presentation.	Low	I'll take a sip of water before the presentation, and I won't even have a glass of water near where I am presenting.
I'll get a standing ovation.	Low	Even if I give a great presentation, the subject is not that exciting!
My classmates will be interested in what I say, and someone will give me a compliment.	High	This happened to me in the past.
I'll have to go to the bathroom in the middle of the presentation.	Low	This has never happened, and I'll use the bathroom before I start.
I'll talk too softly, and someone will ask me to speak up.	Medium	This has happened before, but it wasn't too bad.
I'll forget what I'm supposed to say.	Medium	I'll make sure I have notes on 3x5 index cards in case I forget what to say.
My presentation will go very well, and I'll receive a good grade.	High	This happened to me in the past.
I'll stutter and the class will laugh at me.	Low	This has never happened in the past.
I'll read from my cards without looking up at the class.	Medium	I'll be sure to look up every few seconds and make eye contact with different classmates.

Now try it for yourself.

Possible Outcome	Probability	Reasons/Comments

What thoughts and feelings came to mind when you did this exercise?

Thoughts: _____

_____

_____

_____

_____

Feelings: _____

_____

_____

_____

worksheet

Does Your Worrying Make You Sick?

Objective

To identify the physical symptoms caused by your excessive worrying.

What to Know

If you worry too much, you might have physical problems. Common physical symptoms associated with excessive worrying include:

- Restlessness or feeling on edge
- Easily fatigued
- Muscle tension
- Dizziness
- Headaches
- Stomach problems, including nausea or diarrhea
- Shortness of breath
- Dry mouth
- Rapid heartbeat

Your body experiences worry as stress, producing "stress biochemicals," including cortisol, adrenaline, norepinephrine, and others. When your body is constantly flooded with these biochemicals, you can also experience high blood pressure, a decline in immune system functioning, and a variety of other serious illnesses.

Besides the physical problems that excessive worrying can cause, constant worrying can also lead to habits that cause poor health. These habits include alcohol or drug use, overeating, and sleep problems.

Consider Claire. She can't stop worrying about her family because her parents are divorcing. As a result, she has headaches and stomachaches. Her worries affect her ability to sleep, and she has a hard time waking up on time to get ready for school. She frequently visits the school nurse, who believes that Claire is avoiding class. It hasn't occurred to Claire (or the school nurse and Claire's teachers) that she is experiencing physical problems associated with worry-related stress.

What to Do

Do you think your worrying is affecting you physically? This worksheet is designed to help you identify if your worries are causing physical problems.

Note: *If you have ongoing physical problems, tell your parents or caregivers and see your doctor to find out if there is a medical cause that requires treatment.*

Begin by writing in the physical problems you think are associated with worry and anxiety. Then, note how often they occur: daily, weekly, or monthly. Rate the intensity of your physical problems when you worry, using a scale of 1 to 10, where 1 is "not at all affected by my worrying" and 10 is "always gets worse when I worry." Finally, add any comments regarding how your worrying affects you.

Physical Problem	Frequency	Rating	Comments

Brainstorm ways you can take care of your body in order to decrease physical symptoms associated with your worrying.

Sleep (e.g., turning off your phone and going to sleep at the same time each night):

_____

_____

_____

Exercise (e.g., getting involved with an extracurricular activity or taking a walk each day):

_____

_____

_____

Nutrition (e.g., cutting down on caffeinated drinks):

_____

_____

_____

Relaxation exercises (e.g., using an app to meditate for ten minutes each day):

_____

_____

_____

Are there any other areas in your life where you can make changes?

_____

_____

_____

worksheet

Does Your Anxiety Affect the People Around You?

Objective

To identify how your excessive worrying and anxiety affects the people around you.

What to Know

Most teens with anxiety can't see how their constant worrying is affecting the people around them. But if you find yourself worrying and anxious all the time, then it's almost certain that your state of mind and your behaviors are affecting people around you.

The following are four common ways that your anxiety can affect your relationships. Note that your anxiety can affect your relationships in different ways at different times.

1. **You may be overly dependent.** You might seek constant reassurance from the people around you that everything is going to be okay. You might also require the physical presence of certain people in situations that make you anxious.

2. **You may just want to be alone.** Do you avoid certain social situations or people? If you're ashamed of your worrying or fears, you might find it easier to just be alone.

3. **You might adopt a restricted lifestyle that also restricts those around you.** Do you avoid crowded places or doing things that are unfamiliar? In general, anxious teens seek familiarity and avoid situations where there might be unwanted surprises. This cautious lifestyle affects those around you because they might limit their activities to protect you from getting upset.

4. **You may turn to alcohol or drugs to calm down.** Drugs or alcohol might offer the illusion that you can escape your worries or feel better in the short term. But this can present an entirely new set of problems that will affect you and the people around you.

Consider Chris. She worries about staying safe in her neighborhood. She seeks reassurance from her family, and she constantly checks to see if the doors and windows are locked. She never leaves her home alone after dark, and she avoids spending too much time outside. She used to enjoy playing basketball at the park with her friends, but she no longer goes to the park because of her fears. Her family becomes annoyed and even angry with her because she constantly asks questions to feel reassured. Chris can't seem to stop herself. Can you relate to Chris?

This worksheet is designed to help you put yourself in other people's shoes and consider how your anxiety is affecting them. Avoid feeling guilty about your behavior; this exercise isn't intended to make you feel more anxious! Instead, you will understand how your worries affect the people around you so you can conquer your worries and fears.

What to Do

In the first column, fill in the names of people in your life who are affected by your anxiety, such as your parents or caregivers, siblings, friends, teachers, or relatives. Then, go back and think about how your worrying affects each person and record your answers in the second column. Talk to each person you've listed, asking them how your anxiety affects them, and record their answers in the third column. You might find that your assumptions were correct, but you might also learn that people are not affected in the ways you expected. It's possible that many people close to you are not that aware of your anxiety. Finally, in the last column, write down something you can do differently to change your behavior.

Significant Person/ Relationship	How I Believe My Anxiety Affects That Person	How the Person Said My Anxiety Affects Them	What I Can Do Differently

Name one person in your life who's most affected by your anxiety.

_____

Is this person aware you're trying to overcome anxiety? How is this person helping you?

_____

_____

_____

How do you think life will change for this person if you overcome your anxiety and excessive worrying?

_____

_____

_____

worksheet

Understand Social Anxiety

Objective

To identify and understand the physical, emotional, and mental symptoms of social anxiety.

What to Know

It's normal to feel nervous in some social situations. For example, going on a date or giving a presentation may cause "butterflies" in your stomach. But if you have social anxiety (also called *social phobia*), everyday interactions cause significant anxiety, fear, self-consciousness, and embarrassment because you're afraid of being evaluated or judged by other people. This fear can lead to avoidance that disrupts your life, affecting your daily routine and participation in school or social activities.

Teens with social anxiety experience intense nervousness and self-consciousness in social situations—or sometimes when just thinking about social situations! Often there are accompanying physical symptoms, such as sweating, shaking, upset stomach, or blushing, and these body sensations can intensify anxiety.

If you struggle with social anxiety, you may find that your physical symptoms and fear of humiliation cause you to focus on your own thoughts and feelings rather than on the people around you. You might get caught up in the "what ifs" and self-doubt rather than being aware and involved in what is going on around you. To protect yourself from distress, you might withdraw during social interactions or avoid them altogether.

What to Do

Think about a recent social situation that made you anxious. Rate the symptoms you experienced from 1 to 10, where 1 is "none" and 10 is "very intense."

What was the situation? _____

_____ Muscle tension	_____ Fear
_____ Heart palpitations	_____ Embarrassment
_____ Trembling or shaking	_____ Shame
_____ Sweating	_____ Nervousness
_____ Gasping or shortness of breath	_____ Humiliation
_____ Dizziness	_____ Blushing

_____ Upset stomach or nausea   _____ Feeling that your mind has gone blank

_____ Shaky voice   _____ Little to no eye contact

_____ Numbness or a feeling of disconnection   _____ Chest or neck tightness

_____ Other: _____   _____ Other: _____

What are the top two symptoms you experienced?

_____

_____

Think about a past situation when you experienced those symptoms. Describe what happened.

_____

_____

_____

Since that happened, do you avoid people or situations that make you anxious? _____

Are you worried that you'll experience those symptoms again? _____

Your symptoms can change over time. They may flare up if you are stressed or have increased pressure or demands. Although avoiding situations that produce anxiety might make you feel better in the short term, your anxiety is likely to continue if you don't find ways to cope.

How do you typically deal with your symptoms?

_____

_____

_____

Can you think of tools or resources that can help you cope with social anxiety?

_____

_____

_____

Name one person who can support you in dealing with your social anxiety.

_____

worksheet

How Distressed Are You in Social Situations?

Objective

To identify social situations that cause you the greatest anxiety and rate them using the SUDS (subjective units of distress) scale.

What to Know

If you have social anxiety, you probably avoid situations that cause or increase your distress. You might worry that you'll embarrass yourself or experience uncomfortable physical reactions. Sometimes the fear is mild, but at times it might be paralyzing. Maybe you have heard of an approach called *exposure therapy*, which means that you actually seek out (expose yourself to) the people, places, and situations you fear to overcome your anxiety. It might sound scary at first, but there is a clear method you can follow.

The first step is to identify social situations you fear and then rate them on a special scale called the *SUDS scale*. Later in this workbook you will practice exposing yourself to situations that make you anxious.

What to Do

First, list twenty social situations that make you anxious. (Skip the ratings for now.)

1. _____ SUDS Rating: _____

2. _____ SUDS Rating: _____

3. _____ SUDS Rating: _____

4. _____ SUDS Rating: _____

5. _____ SUDS Rating: _____

6. _____ SUDS Rating: _____

7. _____ SUDS Rating: _____

8. _____ SUDS Rating: _____

9. _____ SUDS Rating: _____

10. _____ SUDS Rating: _____

11. _____ SUDS Rating: _____

12. _____ SUDS Rating: _____

13. _____ SUDS Rating: _____

14. _____ SUDS Rating: _____

15. _____ SUDS Rating: _____

16. _____ SUDS Rating: _____

17. _____ SUDS Rating: _____

18. _____ SUDS Rating: _____

19. _____ SUDS Rating: _____

20. _____ SUDS Rating: _____

Now, review the rating scale that follows. Think about each situation and assign it a number. There is no right answer, and it's based on what you feel *today*, not yesterday or tomorrow or some distant time in the future. This scale can help you understand the severity of your social anxiety and also show you that not every situation is off-the-charts terrifying or paralyzing.

SUDS Scale*

0   No distress; totally relaxed

1   Alert and awake; concentrating well; no real signs of distress

2   Minimal anxiety/distress

3   Mild anxiety/distress; doesn't interfere with functioning

4   Mild to moderate anxiety/distress; you are more aware of your anxiety

5   Moderate anxiety/distress; uncomfortable, but can continue to function

6   Moderate to strong anxiety/distress; you are aware of your anxiety and how it affects you

7   Quite anxious/distressed; interfering with functioning; physiological signs may be present

8   Very anxious/distressed; can't concentrate; physiological signs are present

9   Extremely anxious/distressed; feeling desperate

10 Highest level of distress/fear/anxiety that you have ever felt

As you were listing the social situations that make you anxious, were any of them hard to admit or think about?

_____

_____

_____

Do you hide your anxiety or worry from others? _____

Have you confided in anyone about your difficulties in social situations? _____

Write down the names of trusted adults (e.g., family members, friends, counselors, coaches, teachers) who can help you with this problem.

_____

_____

_____

*Adapted from Back, S. E., Foa, E. B., Killeen, T. K., Mills, K. L., Teesson, M., Dansky Cotton, B., Carroll, K. M., & Brady, K. T. (2014). *Concurrent treatment of PTSD and substance use disorders using prolonged exposure (COPE): Patient workbook.* Oxford University Press.

worksheet

Understand and Track Your Panic Attacks

Objective

To understand what triggers your panic attacks and track them to learn how to manage symptoms.

What to Know

A panic attack is a sudden and sharp rise in anxiety accompanied by physical symptoms such as racing heart, dizziness, numbness, nausea, or shortness of breath. Have you ever had a panic attack? This can be a scary experience, especially since it can occur out of the blue.

You might think: "Am I going crazy? Am I going to die? Am I going to faint or have a heart attack?" These thoughts can trigger even more anxiety, which often leads to worsened symptoms, so it's important to understand that you're not in any danger; your body is overreacting to feeling very anxious. You're experiencing a "false alarm."

If you experience frequent panic attacks, you might constantly worry that you'll have another panic attack, and the anticipation causes you to become even more anxious. Sometimes this worry becomes so intense that you avoid going places where a panic attack might happen, limiting where you feel comfortable going (e.g., attending school, going to the mall, or using public transportation). The more you understand your panic attacks, the closer you'll be to getting rid of them for good. This worksheet is designed to help you understand panic attacks and what triggers your symptoms.

What to Do

The following is a list of common symptoms of panic attacks. Rate the frequency of each symptom from 1 to 10, where 1 is "I do not have this symptom at all" and 10 is "I have this symptom frequently." Additionally, put an asterisk next to the most distressing symptoms you experience.

_____ Palpitations, pounding heart, or accelerated heart rate

_____ Sweating

_____ Trembling or shaking

_____ Shortness of breath or feeling smothered

_____ Feelings of choking

_____ Chest pain or discomfort

_____ Nausea or abdominal pain

_____ Feeling dizzy, unsteady, light-headed, or faint

_____ Chills or heat sensations

_____ Numbness or tingling sensations

_____ Feelings of unreality or that you're going crazy

_____ Feeling detached from yourself (this is called _depersonalization_)

_____ Fear of losing control

_____ Fear of having a heart attack or dying

_____ Sense of danger or impending doom

Next, check off any of the following statements that apply to you.

_____ I experience a fear of places or situations where getting help or escaping might be difficult, such as in a crowd or on a bridge.

_____ I feel unable to travel without a friend or family member.

_____ For at least one month following a panic attack, I have felt persistent concern about having another one.

_____ For at least one month following a panic attack, I have worried about having a heart attack or "going crazy."

_____ For at least one month following a panic attack, I have changed my behavior to avoid another panic attack.

_____ I have had other problems, such as changes in sleeping or eating habits.

_____ I feel sad or depressed more days than not.

_____ I feel disinterested in life more days than not.

_____ I feel worthless or guilty more days than not.

_____ During the last year, I have used alcohol or drugs to deal with my anxiety.

How often do your panic attacks occur? _____

How long do the panic attacks usually last? _____

Describe your typical panic attack, including your thoughts, physical sensations, and feelings.

_____

_____

_____

What usually helps your panic attacks go away?

_____

_____

_____

Use the following chart to track your panic attacks for one month. Rate the severity of your panic attacks from 1 to 10, where 1 is "I wasn't really bothered" and 10 is "severe anxiety; I thought I was going to die."

Date	What Triggered the Attack?	Symptoms You Experienced	Severity (1–10)	What Did You Do to Cope?

Are You Oversensitive to Criticism?

Objective

To identify situations where you are oversensitive to criticism and develop strategies for changing this pattern.

What to Know

Do you let your fear of criticism dominate your life? Sometimes your fear of criticism can keep you from trying new things, taking risks, and getting close to others. It's painful to be oversensitive to criticism, and it's often based on an internalized negative self-view. Perhaps you were shamed or overly criticized when you were very young, and you still view yourself as "small" in relation to other people. For instance, if you get feedback about a class presentation, do you tend to hear only the negative parts and tune out the positive feedback? Do you shut down or lash out when a friend or loved one offers constructive suggestions?

If you're aware that you tend to magnify what might be a mildly negative appraisal of you into a huge personal attack, that's a good thing. Awareness is the first step toward change! It isn't possible to avoid criticism entirely, but you can learn to react and respond in healthier ways. This worksheet will help you reflect on situations that trigger oversensitivity and learn skills to help you cope.

What to Do

On the following lines, describe two situations when you reacted to criticism. Who was involved? What happened? How did you feel, and how did you respond (anger, low self-esteem, irritability, avoidance, etc.)? Then, circle the number of each situation where you might have reacted in an oversensitive way.

1. _____

_____

_____

_____

_____

2. _____

_____

_____

_____

_____

Constructive criticism offers you the opportunity to improve in different areas of your life—at home, at school, and in your community. When you hear criticism, repeat this statement three times aloud: "Criticism can help me in life." How does that feel? Could it change the way you react?

Learning how to lower your reactivity to criticism can take time. Be kind and patient with yourself as you think about and practice the following strategies:

- Listen to what someone is saying with an open mind and try to understand the person's perspective.
- Notice your automatic negative, critical reactions and stop them.
- Repeat to yourself: "I seek improvement, not approval."
- Be assertive—if you've been wrongly criticized, step back, take a breath, and say so.
- Be proactive—if you've made a mistake, approach the person and apologize. If appropriate, ask what you could have done differently.
- Forgive yourself. Repeat phrases such as "I did the best I could," "I'm going to make mistakes sometimes—everyone does," or "I'm not a bad person for making a mistake."
- Let it go. Stop obsessing or worrying about what happened.
- Practice self-compassion by changing your inner talk to match what you would say to a loved one or friend.
- See the value in another's criticism. What can you learn from this experience? Ask for clarity, if required.
- Try not to become defensive or offer a "counter critique." Step away and rethink your response.
- If you're upset, ask to postpone the conversation.
- Take deep breaths, or find other ways to calm yourself.
- Thank the person offering feedback—even if it was not helpful or constructive!

Pick one situation from your list. Describe how you would like to deal with that type of situation in the future. Consider how the criticism was helpful and why you might have been oversensitive.

_____

_____

_____

_____

_____

_____

worksheet

Are You Afraid to Be Away from Your Parents or Caregivers?

Objective

To decrease your anxiety about being away from your parents or caregivers.

What to Know

As you grow older and more independent, you are likely doing more and more things apart from your parents or caregivers. You might feel excitement, even if it makes you nervous. When you think about being apart from your parents or caregivers, you might feel anxious to the point of not wanting to leave home at all. You might even experience physical symptoms, such as headaches, nausea, dizziness, stomachaches, sleep problems, or other discomfort.

You might try to hide your worry or ignore it because you think some people might say, "You're too old for that" or "What's the big deal? Don't be a baby." This only makes matters worse because pushing away your true feelings doesn't work. Do you find yourself in a cycle of worry when it comes to being apart from your parents or caregivers? If so, there's good news: You can learn skills and strategies for managing separation anxiety.

One skill you can use is called *mindfulness*. Mindfulness can help you disengage from your worries and fears that something bad will happen if you're away from your parents or caregivers. We'll learn about mindfulness later in this book. But first, let's get a better picture of what is happening to you now.

What to Do

Check off any of the symptoms in the following list that you have experienced when you were apart from your parents or caregivers, such as going to school or camp, or staying home while they were out. Put an asterisk next to the symptom that's most distressing.

_____ Stomachache

_____ Dizziness

_____ Racing heart

_____ Shallow breathing

_____ Headache

_____ Heart palpitations

_____ Shortness of breath

_____ Panic attack

_____ Pain in any part of your body

_____ Inability to sleep

What situations typically trigger these physical symptoms? How long do they last? What helps you deal with the symptoms, if anything?

_____

_____

_____

Name your fears and worries related to being apart from your parents or caregivers.

_____

_____

_____

To get more information about your worries, use the following chart to track the specific situations that trigger you when you're apart from your parent or caregiver. Describe your thoughts, feelings, and behaviors at these times, and rate your level of distress on a scale of 1 to 10, where 1 is "very little distress" and 10 is "the worst distress you've ever experienced."

Trigger Situation	Thoughts, Feelings, and Behaviors	Level of Distress (1–10)

As you learn to manage your fears and worries with the tools in this book, you might try "trial separations" where you purposely and gradually spend more and more time away from your parents or caregivers.

Do You Have Health Anxiety?

Objective

To identify if your physical symptoms are related to anxiety and stress.

What to Know

Getting sick is common for teens, from strep throat to the flu. Usually a trip to the doctor, some medicine, and a few days in bed is enough to feel better. But if you worry about each ache and pain and wonder if it's a serious illness, you may have something called *health anxiety*. For example, you may have a headache and worry that it's a brain tumor, or you may have a stomachache and wonder if it's appendicitis.

It's more likely that physical symptoms aren't a life-threatening illness, but are just normal body sensations. Ironically, the stress and worry you feel about your health can make your symptoms increase and worsen. This constant worry can also contribute to trouble sleeping, loss of appetite, and difficulty concentrating at school.

Here are some of the signs of health anxiety. Put a check next to any that describe you.

_____ I worry that any physical discomfort I have is a sign of a serious illness.

_____ I'm always checking myself for any sign of illness.

_____ I often ask my parent or caregiver to take me the doctor.

_____ I frequently ask my parent or caregiver to take my temperature.

_____ I think about and talk about my health constantly.

_____ I often find lumps that no one else can feel.

_____ I frequently visit the school nurse.

_____ When I'm at school, I spend a lot of time in the bathroom because I feel sick.

_____ I'm afraid to be around people who are sick.

Sometimes teens develop physical symptoms *because* they are anxious or worried. A teen who is stressed out about a class presentation may develop stomach issues, including nausea and diarrhea. A teen who is being bullied at school may be worried about getting beat up between classes and develop headaches that cause them to miss school for several days. These are real physical symptoms that develop from excess worry and anxiety.

What to Do

Your thoughts and worries about illness are just thoughts. They aren't always a sign that something is actually wrong with you. Using the following chart, track your health worries. Describe your symptoms and note when they occur. Explain what you think might be wrong with you, and then rank how likely a diagnosis is to happen on a scale of 1 to 10, where 1 is "not likely to happen" and 10 is "definitely will happen." Finally, come up with other explanations for your symptoms.

What Are Your Symptoms and When Do They Occur?	What Do You Think Is Wrong with You?	Is a Diagnosis Likely? (1–10)	What Could Be Another Cause of Your Symptoms?

worksheet

How Do Avoidance Behaviors Impact Your Life?

Objective

To stop avoiding the places, people, and objects you fear by identifying your avoidance behaviors.

What to Know

Do you avoid going to the mall because you worry you'll catch the flu? Do you insist that your friends drive because you worry you'll get into an accident or hit an animal or person? Do you refuse to take the bus, or are you afraid to fly in an airplane? Do your fears make your life miserable or cause you to miss out on wonderful experiences that could make your life better?

You might not recognize these behaviors as compulsive, but they are. A compulsion is any act that's performed as a result of an irresistible urge to behave in a certain way, especially when it's against your conscious wishes. Compulsions are usually thought of as obvious acts, such as repeatedly checking locks or excessively washing your hands. But avoidance is also a type of compulsive behavior. You might believe that avoiding certain places, objects, and people will keep you safe.

Over time, you'll find that your sense of fear will increase because you never give yourself the opportunity to see if you can deal with uncomfortable situations, or learn whether your conclusions about what's safe (or not) are accurate.

What to Do

Review the examples provided, circling any objects or situations that you avoid, and add other things you avoid.

Places: public restrooms, malls, schools, public parks, hospitals, airports, train stations, swimming pools, meeting places, any crowded area

Other: _____

People and animals: dogs, cats, birds, spiders, insects, relatives, children or babies, classmates, teachers, doctors, dentists, people who are or who have been sick

Other: _____

Objects: various colors, cars, pencils, pens, shoes, diapers, dirty clothes, numbers or letters, specific images, paper, garbage

Other: _____

Situations: driving or riding in a car, riding in a bus or train, flying on an airplane, being physically close to sick people, being in a crowd, coming in close contact with certain numbers or colors that you consider unlucky, being around certain animals or insects, going places by yourself

Other: _____

For the next two weeks, use the chart to identify places, people, animals, objects, and situations you avoid because they make you anxious. Rate your anxiety level on a scale of 1 to 10, where 1 is "low anxiety" and 10 is "the most extreme anxiety you've experienced."

Date	What Did You Avoid?	Anxiety Level (1–10)	Describe Your Thoughts, Feelings, and Physical Symptoms

What did you avoid the most? _____

Who or what can help you stop this behavior? For example, you might ask your counselor or therapist for help, or gradually spend more time in situations you usually avoid.

_____

_____

_____

worksheet

Are You Too Rigid About Routines and Schedules?

Objective

To identify your rigid habits, patterns, routines, and schedules and explore strategies for less rigidity and more spontaneity in your life.

What to Know

Routines, schedules, and daily plans are a great way for you to meet your obligations, fulfill your responsibilities, and pave the way for success and creativity. Following certain patterns of behavior over and over again can contribute to establishing a healthy lifestyle for a lifetime. For instance, if you never miss your 6:00 a.m. workout before school, you're performing a routine that contributes to your health and happiness.

But if you feel so compelled to stick to your routines and schedules that you experience anxiety or distress at the thought of interrupting or changing them, this can be a problem. You might be trying to control emotionally challenging situations that make you anxious or upset.

In this worksheet, you'll explore what your routines and habits are, as well as their consequences, and review some strategies for making changes.

What to Do

Describe your regular routines you feel you *must* follow, or you will feel anxious or upset. Write whatever comes to mind, no matter how minor or insignificant it might seem—for instance, brushing your teeth at a certain time, organizing your clothes or other items in a certain way, and so on.

_____

_____

_____

_____

What are the positive gains of your rigid adherence to those routines?

_____

_____

_____

_____

What are the negative consequences of your rigid adherence to those routines?

_____

_____

_____

_____

What do you feel might happen if you interrupt the routines you listed? Be specific.

_____

_____

_____

_____

Choose one of the routines you listed. What's one small way you can alter it to start reducing your need for rigid routines?

_____

_____

_____

_____

worksheet

Do You Have Depression Along with Anxiety?

Objective

To identify if you have depression along with anxiety and plan at least two pleasurable activities each day to increase your motivation and lift your mood.

What to Know

If you have anxiety, you might also have symptoms of depression. These two problems are very different, but they do share some symptoms. Coping skills and tools for anxiety are often recommended if you have depression. The presence of depressive symptoms may lead to an increase in anxiety symptoms, and vice versa.

If you struggle with anxiety, you're at an increased risk of developing depression. If you struggle with both depression and anxiety, most likely you suffered with anxiety first, and the depression developed sometime later. The likelihood of depression developing after anxiety could be due to the impact that ongoing anxious thoughts can have on your mental health and overall outlook on life. This seems to be particularly true if you have panic disorder, as panic attacks tend to trigger feelings of fear, helplessness, and catastrophe.

Both depression and anxiety cause nervousness, insomnia, irritability, and lack of focus. But depression includes a different set of symptoms that need to be addressed. It affects how you think, feel, and behave, and it can cause emotional, functional, and physical problems. These are the common symptoms of depression:

- Feelings of sadness for no apparent reason
- Crying spells
- Frustration or anger over small issues
- Feeling hopeless or empty
- Irritable or annoyed mood
- Loss of interest or pleasure in activities
- Loss of interest in, or conflict with, family and friends
- Low self-esteem
- Feelings of worthlessness or guilt
- Focus on past failures

- Exaggerated self-blame or self-criticism
- Extreme sensitivity to rejection or failure
- Need for excessive reassurance
- Difficulty thinking, concentrating, making decisions, and remembering things
- Frequent thoughts of death, dying, or suicide
- Tiredness and low energy
- Insomnia or sleeping too much
- Changes in appetite
- Alcohol or drug use
- Agitation or restlessness
- Slowed thinking, speaking, or body movements
- Complaints of unexplained body aches and headaches
- Social isolation
- Poor school performance or frequent absences from school
- Less attention to personal hygiene or appearance
- Disruptive or risky behaviors
- Self-harm

Note: *If you have suicidal thoughts, immediately seek help. Call the National Suicide Prevention Hotline at 800-273-8255.*

What to Do

This worksheet will address one of the most common problems associated with depression: the inability to do fun or pleasurable activities. Planning your day so it includes enjoyable activities can help motivate you to spend more time doing things that will lift your mood and bring purpose to your life.

Write down an activity that always makes you smile. _____

Write down an activity that always relaxes you. _____

Write down an activity that you do with other people. _____

Write down an activity that stimulates your thinking. _____

Write down an activity that makes you proud of yourself. _____

Write down an activity that brings back wonderful memories. _____

Write down an activity that is always fun. _____

Write down other activities that give your life meaning and purpose.

_____

_____

On the following chart, schedule at least two pleasurable activities each day. Plan activities that you know are possible to do and require relatively little effort. After the activity, rate your mood 1 to 10, where 1 is "sad and hopeless" and 10 is "happy with my life." Add comments about each activity. Make copies of this chart and fill it in every day for at least two weeks.

Time	Activity	Rating	Comments
7 a.m.			
8 a.m.			
9 a.m.			
10 a.m.			
11 a.m.			
Noon			
1 p.m.			
2 p.m.			
3 p.m.			
4 p.m.			
5 p.m.			
6 p.m.			
7 p.m.			
8 p.m.			
9 p.m.			
10 p.m.			
11 p.m.			

What did you find most challenging about this activity?

_____

_____

_____

Did you experience an increase in anxiety when engaging in activities? Explain.

_____

_____

_____

Did doing two activities each day lift your mood and increase your motivation? Why or why not?

_____

_____

_____

Think of people, resources, or tools that can help you plan fun activities. List them.

_____

_____

_____

What did you learn from this exercise?

_____

_____

_____

How Anxiety Affects Your Social and Academic Life—and What To Do About It!

section 2

Identify Your Worst Fears About Social Situations

Objective

To identify your fears about the worst things that could happen to you in social situations.

What to Know

You might not fully understand what causes you to avoid social situations. Maybe you automatically become anxious before certain situations occur, such as attending parties, going on a date, presenting in class, or even being asked for your opinion. Before the situation or activity, you might plot your escape route, imagine excuses for not showing up, or spin a web of catastrophic thoughts about all the bad things that might happen. This reaction is called *anticipatory anxiety*.

Most teens have some degree of nervousness in anticipation of certain situations, but for teens with social anxiety, the anticipation itself can become crippling and interfere with getting through each day.

It's important to recognize that as scary as these thoughts are, they are just thoughts. Nothing bad is actually happening in the moment. If you have social anxiety, the worry and fear are so ingrained that the anxious thoughts are like a reflex. Sometimes physical responses kick in, too. You might notice your heart beating faster. You might start sweating or feel like you can't breathe. The "what-if" thoughts start churning about all the things that could go wrong, causing you to feel sick to your stomach. Does this sound like you?

The great news is, if you identify your thoughts and fears in advance of social situations, you can slowly gain confidence and discover that your worst fears won't actually come true!

What to Do

In this worksheet, you'll clarify your worst fears about social situations. Before you do this exercise, be sure you are in a place where you feel safe and where you're unlikely to be interrupted. Let your imagination run wild while knowing that nothing bad is happening in the present moment. If you experience some anxiety, that's normal. Just take some breaths and keep going.

Close your eyes and imagine yourself in the following situations. Really put yourself in the situation in your mind as much as you are able. Then, write down your worst fears related to that situation. You could also draw an image of the fear. For example, in the first scenario, someone might write: "If my teacher asks for my opinion, my worst fear is that I'll start blushing and stammering; then, I'll feel like I can't breathe and I won't be able to talk at all. I'll start to panic and have to leave the room to throw up in the bathroom, if I even make it that far. Then, I'll never be able to look anyone in the eye again, and eventually they'll know what a basket case I am."

You're in class and your teacher unexpectedly asks you to share your opinion about the subject under discussion.

_____

_____

_____

You're invited to attend a surprise party for a friend, but you find out most of the people there are strangers.

_____

_____

_____

You're asked to go out to eat with a friend, as well as some people you don't know.

_____

_____

_____

Your best friend sets you up on a blind date with someone you think you might like.

_____

_____

_____

You're out with friends and need to use a public restroom.

_____

_____

_____

You have to take an important test.

_____

_____

_____

Describe a situation of your own that causes you anticipatory anxiety.

_____

_____

_____

_____

_____

_____

_____

What's the worst thing you imagine will happen in this situation?

_____

_____

_____

What's the best thing that could happen in this situation?

_____

_____

_____

What's the most likely thing that will happen in this situation?

_____

_____

_____

worksheet

Are You Avoiding School?

Objective

To understand the reasons behind your school avoidance and identify strategies for coping with your feelings.

What to Know

Some teens struggle to get to school on a regular basis. Does that describe you? Perhaps you're shy, anxious, or depressed. Maybe you feel "different," or you're upset about something that happened at school. Perhaps you've been bullied or criticized but you haven't told anyone. Maybe there are problems at home—such as divorce, illness, trauma, or arguing—that make it difficult to leave home to go to school. Perhaps you're feeling excluded by, or competitive with, other kids. There could be many reasons why you avoid going to school.

If you avoid going to school, you probably aren't trying to "get out of doing something." Instead, you're probably trying to cope with overwhelming emotions that make you want to retreat and avoid dealing with them. That's understandable, but it can cause negative consequences in your life, such as school failure, loss of self-esteem, and ongoing anxiety or depression.

Rather than avoiding the worries and fears that arise when you need to go to school, it's important for you to face your worries in a planned, safe way.

What to Do

Answer the following questions as honestly as you can.

How often do you miss school? _____

What are the main reasons you miss school? (Reasons might include illness, family problems, depression, anxiety, bullying, shyness, relationship problems, peer teasing, teacher criticism, and so on.)

_____

_____

_____

_____

Are there any particular people you are trying to avoid? Name them and explain why.

_____

_____

_____

_____

What are the positive effects of avoiding your peers and/or teachers at school? For example, you might say you feel safer, you avoid conflict, or you feel less depressed.

_____

_____

_____

_____

What are the negative consequences of avoiding your peers and/or teachers at school? For example, your grades might be poor, your parents might get upset, or you might feel lonely or "stupid."

_____

_____

_____

_____

Here are some strategies for dealing with skipping school to avoid teachers or peers:

- Practice mindfulness. When you're mindful, you notice what's happening right here and now without judgment and with acceptance. You can learn to not worry so much about things that have happened in the past or things that have not yet happened. You can learn to accept your feelings rather than try to run away from them. Be kind and compassionate to yourself.

- Learn relaxation and meditation techniques. Calming yourself when you're upset or anxious is a skill that you can use for the rest of your life. Check out apps such as www. insighttimer.com, www.headspace.com, or www.happify.com, or find others that work for you.

- Understand your thoughts and worries are just that—ideas in your head that might not actually be true.

- Try exposure therapy by gradually facing the thing that you're avoiding with support from someone safe. You might go to school *while* you're anxious and even experience an increase in anxiety while you're there, but it doesn't need to be a catastrophe. You can practice deep breathing. Tell yourself reassuring statements, like "I can do this!" "Nothing bad is happening," "I'm going to be okay," and so on. Take it one step at a time.

- Set up a reward system with your family. For instance, you earn a privilege or small gift if you go to school. This can be motivating, but you should also continue working on your fears.

What are the first steps you'll take to address your school avoidance?

_____

_____

_____

What obstacles might get in the way of addressing this problem?

_____

_____

_____

Name one or two people you trust who can help you work on this problem.

_____

_____

How to Handle School Pressure

Objective

To increase coping strategies to lessen the pressure to do well in school.

What to Know

Even for the most organized, motivated, and rested student, school pressure can sometimes pile up so much that it can be overwhelming. In addition to trying to keep up with your schoolwork, you might be juggling extracurricular activities, a part-time job, and your social and family life. You might be pressuring yourself, or you might have parents who push you hard. You might be dealing with teachers with high expectations, or you might be experiencing a combination of all of these!

Stress is not always a bad thing—it can motivate you to act. But too much stress can result in negative consequences, such as headaches, anxiety, depression, insomnia, substance abuse, or eating disorders. When you become overwhelmed, it can be hard to focus or set priorities, and then you might fall behind on your tasks and responsibilities.

It's never too late to figure out how to handle academic pressure and stress. If you learn strategies now, they can serve you throughout your education and into your adult working life, too.

What to Do

In this worksheet, you will look at the things causing stress in your life and then review strategies for lowering your school-related stress. Answer the following questions to the best of your ability.

What are the *main* sources of school pressure or stress that you feel right now? Be sure to identify specific *internal sources* (e.g., your desire to achieve and excel, perfectionism, fear of failure) as well as *external sources* (e.g., pressure from your parents, teachers, or coaches).

_____

_____

_____

_____

Are there other sources of school pressure that you're experiencing right now?

_____

_____

What negative effects are you experiencing related to school pressure or stress?

Physical:

_____

_____

Emotional/psychological:

_____

_____

Social:

_____

_____

Family:

_____

_____

Financial:

_____

_____

Other:

_____

_____

How are you dealing with those negative effects?

_____

_____

_____

Here are some ideas for how to manage school pressure and related stress:

- Listen to your thoughts, but don't let them take control. They are just thoughts, and they don't need to determine your actions all the time.
- Lower your own high expectations or demands to be perfect. Unattainable goals can lead to burnout and disappointment. Sometimes it's okay to aim for "good enough."
- If your parents or caregivers are particularly demanding, find a quiet time to talk openly with them about how stress is affecting you. If you need help, talk to another person you trust, such as a sibling, teacher, or guidance counselor.
- Make a to-do list and mark which items are high, medium, or low priority. Focus on the high-priority items first.
- Organize your workspace, whether that's a table, a desk, or your bed. Clear away the clutter so you can focus on your work. Keep the supplies you need handy.
- Review your schedule and consider cutting out unimportant activities or obligations.
- Tackle tasks one step at a time; avoid "fast-forwarding" or obsessing about all the things you *haven't* done yet.
- Take care of yourself! Eat healthy meals, exercise, take breaks, and learn to meditate or practice yoga.
- Limit your caffeine use. Too much coffee, caffeinated sodas, or energy drinks can cause irritation and agitation.
- Do something relaxing.
- Schedule fun activities unrelated to schoolwork or grades.
- Get enough sleep! The brain is still developing during adolescence, and your body is going through hormonal changes. Sleep deprivation is a key cause of burnout and stress among teens.
- Take breaks from your devices. Yes, this is a hard one, but constant exposure to media of all kinds affects the nervous system. You might install a "block" or "break" app to remove distractions. Set a curfew for texting or other electronic activities every night. And ask for help—finding a buddy to do this with can make it a lot easier.

What is the first step you'd like to take to deal with school pressure?

_____

_____

_____

Name two activities you're willing to try in the next week to help you manage your school stress.

1. _____

2. _____

Who are two or three people you feel comfortable talking to about your school pressure?

_____

_____

_____

Do You Worry About Your Grades?

Objective

To identify when you are worrying excessively about your grades and learn a technique to decrease your worrying.

What to Know

Some students are so anxious about their grades that they have trouble sleeping, eating, and concentrating. Some experience physical problems like stomachaches or headaches. Some even start using alcohol and drugs to cope with the stress.

A little worrying is perfectly normal, but excessive worrying about grades can cause lots of other problems, and your worrying doesn't help. You might even find yourself spending so much time worrying about your grades that it keeps you from studying, and obviously that's not what you want.

This worksheet will help you identify whether you're worrying so much about your grades that your anxiety has become a problem. You will also learn a technique to deal with constant worries that cause distress.

Note: *Some people have a tendency to worry more than others, but you don't have to let your worries run your life. If you worry about a lot of things, not just grades, make sure that an adult you trust (such as a parent or caregiver, teacher, or counselor) knows this is a problem for you.*

What to Do

You'll know that you're worrying too much about grades when you have constant worries and you can't let them go. We call these worries "intrusive thoughts" because they intrude on your normal activities, just like a pesky gnat might bother you.

The following five steps can help you deal with excessive and intrusive worries about your grades. *The general idea is not to fight these worries and try to get rid of them, but rather just accept them for what they are.* When you learn to accept your worries rather than resist them, you will find they become less important in your life.

1. Label your worries as "just thoughts." You can be aware of your worries about grades, but understand they are just thoughts you're having. You don't have to respond to them. What does this mean? Imagine that you're looking at Instagram and you notice an image of a terrible storm. You could stop what you're doing and start thinking about this storm.

You could imagine yourself in the storm, thinking about getting wet and blown around. You could imagine the storm blowing down trees, even tearing apart your home—or worse. But you probably wouldn't do this. You would just scroll on to another image. After all, the image is just an image. It has no power. *And your thoughts about grades have no power over you either. Your worries are just thoughts.*

2. Tell yourself these thoughts are just your brain on "automatic," and you can ignore them.

3. Accept and allow the thoughts into your mind. Don't try to push them away.

4. Breathe from your belly until your anxiety starts to decrease.

5. Continue whatever you were doing prior to your worries.

Use the following chart to track how successful you are at using the 5-step technique. Enter the date. Rate the severity of your worrying from 1 to 10, where 1 is "not much at all" and 10 is "I can't think of anything else but my grades." Indicate whether you used the 5-step technique with Y (yes) or N (no). List how many minutes and seconds it took you to resume what you were doing after your worrying started. If you used the 5-step technique, describe which steps you used, and rate how much you felt in control, where 1 is "I felt in complete control of my worries" and 10 is "my worries totally controlled me."

Date	Worrying Severity (1–10)	Used the 5-Step Technique? (Y/N)	Time to Resume Activity (M:S)	How Did You Stop Your Intrusive Worrying? (Which Steps?)	Feelings of Control (1–10)

worksheet

Feel Less Anxious When Taking Tests

Objective

To use breathing techniques to feel less anxious when taking tests.

What to Know

Taking tests can be stressful, even when you've studied and prepared. Many students worry about how they will do on an exam, no matter how confident they are or how much they've studied. But sometimes normal worry can turn into something called *test anxiety*, which can make it impossible to concentrate and remember information. The following are some of the symptoms of test anxiety. Have you experienced any of them?

- Physical symptoms such as headache, fast heartbeat, shortness of breath, and nausea
- Feeling overwhelmed and forgetting everything you studied
- Negative thoughts, such as believing you will fail the exam
- Second-guessing yourself as you answer questions or changing your answers repeatedly

What happens when you take a test? Describe your thoughts, feelings, and body sensations.

_____

_____

_____

Are there other anxiety symptoms you have experienced before or during a test?

_____

_____

_____

What to Do

There are things you can do to reduce your anxiety before a test, such as exercising to burn off excess energy, getting a good a night's sleep the night before, and, of course, being well-prepared for the test by studying and practicing.

During the exam itself, a breathing exercise can help. Follow these steps:

1. Breathe in through your nose as you count to 4.
2. Exhale through your mouth as you count to 8.
3. Repeat a positive statement to yourself, such as "I can do this. I am prepared."
4. Visualize yourself finishing the test, feeling confident that you have done a good job.
5. Return your attention to the test.
6. Repeat this exercise again, if necessary.

Practice this breathing technique five or six times before a test, while studying, or while doing your homework. Then, use the technique when you actually take a test. Use the following chart to write down changes that you notice while doing the breathing exercise.

Date of the Test	Type of Test	How I Felt Before the Breathing Exercise	How I Felt During the Exercise	How I Felt After the Exercise

Did you find that your test anxiety decreased over time? Explain how the breathing technique affected your anxiety.

_____

_____

_____

What other activities do you find helpful for relieving stress before taking tests?

_____

_____

_____

Describe other situations when you feel anxious and the breathing exercise might help.

_____

_____

_____

Feel Less Anxious During School Presentations

Objective

To reduce your anxiety about making school presentations.

What to Know

Are you afraid to make presentations in school? You're not alone. For many students, standing in front of the class and being the center of attention can cause anxiety, fear, or panic. You might be worried about being laughed at by your classmates. You could have concerns about stammering or forgetting what you were going to say, or letting your classmates see your nervousness. You could be afraid of having a physical reaction that everyone will see, such as fainting, vomiting, or sweating.

Giving presentations in front of your teacher and classmates is a required part of your schoolwork. If you're planning to go to college, your professors will most likely assign presentations. Additionally, you may end up working in an occupation where giving presentations to your team or your customers is an expected task. So, since giving presentations is unavoidable, what can you do?

First, acknowledge that some fear and discomfort is normal—and this includes some physical side effects, such as sweating, blushing, or dry mouth. Next, consider the more you do something, the less scary it becomes. While avoiding a situation might make you feel better in the short term, it has long-lasting consequences. The situation tends to feel even bigger and scarier the next time it comes around, causing your anxiety to increase even more. When you can stay in a situation even though it makes you feel anxious, you will stop the cycle of anxiety.

What to Do

Exposure therapy helps you adjust to situations you fear so you can overcome your anxiety. So, the more you give presentations or speak in front of groups, the less frightening it will become. Here are some small steps you can take to get started.

- Raise your hand to be called on when your teacher asks a question, or ask a question of your own.
- Volunteer to do an exercise or demonstration in front of the class.

- Walk into class after most of your classmates are seated so that most of them will be looking at you.
- Talk, sing, or play an instrument in front of a small group of your friends.
- Share your fear with others. Tell a few trusted classmates that you're anxious about the presentation, and ask them to help you practice.
- Other idea: _____

Now, follow these steps.

1. Select several activities from the list.
2. Rate the activities on a scale of 1 to 10, with 10 being the highest level of anxiety.
3. Expose yourself to the activities, starting with the one with the lowest anxiety ranking.
4. Rate the situation again after the exposure.
5. Increase your tolerance by selecting the next highest anxiety ranking, and continue through the list until you are exposed to the activity with the number closest to 10.

Activity	Anxiety Level Before Exposure (1–10)	Anxiety Level After Exposure (1–10)	How I Feel Now

What are my biggest fears about this presentation?

_____

_____

_____

What is the worst that can happen if these fears came true?

_____

_____

_____

Understanding that your fears are about the worst things that could happen, what is the *most likely* thing that could happen?

_____

_____

_____

How do you think you will feel once you are done with the presentation?

_____

_____

_____

Once you have practiced exposing yourself to situations where you might be anxious in front of others, use the following chart to record your anxiety levels from 1 to 10, where 1 is "very little anxiety" and 10 is "the worst anxiety you've ever experienced during real presentations."

Type (Name) of Presentation	Date	Anxiety Level Before (1–10)	Anxiety Level After (1–10)

worksheet

Missing Out Because You're Anxious

Objective

To identify and practice tolerating situations that trigger social anxiety to decrease feelings of missing out.

What to Know

If you have social anxiety, usual, expected, and normal social situations almost always trigger fear or anxiety. Your fears are generally out of proportion to the situation. You might know that your fears are unreasonable and that other people don't feel the same way. You might feel alone and believe that no one understands you—and you might often feel left out.

If you frequently avoid situations that make you uncomfortable, and you feel self-conscious and distressed because of this avoidance, you might feel like you are missing out.

What to Do

Here are some common situations you might avoid because they make you anxious. Check off each statement that applies to you. Put an asterisk next to any situations that make you feel like you're missing out.

_____ Working with a group of peers to complete a class project

_____ Writing on a whiteboard or chalkboard at the front of the classroom

_____ Walking through crowded hallways

_____ Using public bathrooms

_____ Talking to people you don't know

_____ Taking tests

_____ Starting or joining conversations

_____ Speaking to adults

_____ Participating in physical education class or sports

_____ Performing on stage in front of a crowd

_____ Asking a group of friends to get together or inviting your peers to a party

_____ Having your photo taken

_____ Asking someone out on a date

_____ Reading aloud in front of the class

_____ Eating in front of other people

_____ Entering a room where other people are already seated

_____ Attending parties, dances, or other school activities

_____ Answering questions in class

_____ Talking on the telephone

_____ Asking teachers questions or asking for help

_____ Going to the mall or other crowded places

Based on your selections, write down situations that commonly make you anxious, and rate how uncomfortable _thinking_ about the situation makes you, where 1 is "just a little uncomfortable" and 10 is "extremely anxious."

Situation	Rating

Now, choose one of the activities you listed and practice this activity for one month. Rate your level of anxiety before and after, and record the number of minutes you spent practicing the activity. Write down your thoughts in the final column.

	Rating Before (1–10)	Situation	Rating After (1–10)	Minutes Spent	Notes
Week 1					
Week 2					
Week 3					
Week 4					

Understand How Social Media Affects Your Social Anxiety

Objective

To understand how social media contributes to anxiety and identify ways to develop more social relationships in the real world.

What to Know

If you have social anxiety, you might avoid social situations and become isolated. With social media as an acceptable way of communicating 24/7, you now have even more ways and more excuses to avoid being around other people.

Oddly enough, the increase in the use of social media can actually increase your anxiety. Depression and anxiety, especially among teens, are associated with spending too much time online. Do you measure your self-esteem by the "likes" and comments you receive? Do you believe that the more followers someone has, the happier they are? If you use social media to compare yourself to others and their seemingly perfect lives, this might be a recipe for increased anxiety.

There are benefits to social media: information and photo sharing, venting feelings, getting support, and more. But people with social anxiety are prone to hiding out on social media, which can be a form of escaping real life. So, even though the use of technology can be a coping mechanism for social anxiety, it may also cause your anxiety to worsen because it isn't dealt with.

Overcoming social anxiety can best be achieved through repeated in-person practice with other people. The less you practice social skills, the harder it is to improve those skills. In this worksheet, you will evaluate your social media use, learn some alternatives to using social media, and reflect on your next steps.

What to Do

Write down the devices, applications, and modes of communication you use on a regular basis (e.g., smartphone, Snapchat, texting), and estimate how much time you spend per day on each. For help in assessing your device time, you might want to install a time-tracking app such as Moment or OFFTIME to gather data.

Device/App/Mode of Communication   **Estimated Time Spent Daily**

_____   _____

_____   _____

_____   _____

_____   _____

_____   _____

_____   _____

What are the positive effects of your technology use, such sharing thoughts and feelings?

_____

_____

_____

What are the negative effects of your technology use, such as lack of face-to-face time or difficulty having an in-person conversation without interruption?

_____

_____

_____

Now, for the negative effects you listed, think about how you can change your use of technology. Here are some ideas:

- Schedule social activities that feel safe to you, such as small group gatherings with friends.
- Go to a concert, movie, or sporting event.
- When you feel anxious, instead of reaching for your phone, move your body. Walk, go up and down stairs, or activate your body to bring oxygen to your brain.
- Make an effort to be social in small groups without using your phones. Make eye contact with others and engage in "low-risk" small talk about mutually comfortable subjects.
- Practice sharing, in person, your thoughts and feelings with friends and loved ones. Resist the urge to hide behind the safety and anonymity of texting or emails.
- Plan to reduce the time you spend on devices. Set a goal of limiting tech use to a specific number of minutes per day. Then, stick to it.

- Alternatively, *schedule in* your use of technology.
- Install a blocking app that restricts your access to social media.
- Shut off all devices an hour before bedtime.
- Make time to be in nature, such as cycling, walking, hiking, or running with friends.
- Take a meditation or yoga class.
- Go to the gym.

What changes are you willing to try in the next week or so? (You can use your own ideas, too!)

_____

_____

_____

Now, each day, schedule alternatives to spending time on your devices. Rate your anxiety before doing the activity, where 1 is "just a little uncomfortable" and 10 is "extremely anxious." After you spend time completely away from your devices, rate your anxiety again. Calculate the total time you're away from your devices each day.

Date	Anxiety Before (1–10)	Activity	Anxiety After (1–10)	Total Time Away from Tech Devices

Which alternatives to using technology were the easiest and most fun for you, and why?

_____

_____

_____

Which alternatives seem the most challenging, and why?

_____

_____

_____

Of the easy and the challenging alternatives that you identified, which ones can you commit to scheduling, despite any resistance you might feel?

_____

_____

_____

How anxious were you during the time you were away from your tech devices?

_____

_____

_____

Did you notice a decrease in your anxiety as the week progressed? Describe any changes you experienced.

_____

_____

_____

Reduce Your Self-Consciousness in Social Situations

Objective

To practice ways to manage self-consciousness in social situations.

What to Know

Teens with social anxiety often feel that everyone is evaluating their every word and their every movement. However, if you were to actually poll the people you fear are observing and judging you, the majority of them would likely say they're not. In fact, in many cases, they might say they didn't even notice you.

Believe it or not, even if other people *are* judging you, it doesn't mean they're right, and it shouldn't affect your self-image.

Teens who are very self-conscious usually focus their attention inward, to the exclusion of noticing what's going on around them. You might be acutely aware of your physical sensations or symptoms, such as blushing or a racing heart. You might notice that you are fidgety or restless. You might experience embarrassment or shame. You might also feel unsafe or exposed, and you might have the urge to escape to the safety of being alone, which provides temporary relief from your anxiety.

What to Do

In this worksheet, you'll learn the skills to become less self-conscious in social situations and replace your self-consciousness with *curiosity and self-compassion.*

Think about a situation when you felt highly self-conscious or embarrassed, and answer the following questions.

What was the situation? _____

When did it take place? _____

Were you by yourself or with someone? _____

How did you feel? _____

_____

_____

Now you are going to go out "in the field" to gather data. Choose a public setting where you don't know anyone (so you aren't risking being judged or scrutinized by someone you might see again). Bring this worksheet with you, and find a place where you can sit or stand while writing your notes.

First, focus for at least four or five minutes on yourself and consider the following questions: What are you feeling? What kinds of thoughts are you noticing? Are any memories or images coming up?

_____

_____

_____

_____

_____

Now, focus your attention outward. Notice the people. Pick one or two people to observe (without being too obvious about it). What do you notice about each person? How are they dressed? What do you imagine their mood is? Do they seem to have a lot of energy or not? Do they seem engaged in what they are doing or distracted? If the situation allows, you might say something innocuous to that person ("Nice day, don't you think?" "Looks like it's going to snow," "How about that game last night?"). See what that feels like and write down your observations, focusing on what you noticed and what you felt.

_____

_____

_____

_____

_____

_____

What was different between the first part, when you were focusing on yourself, and the next part, when you were focusing on other people? What was the same? Was one experience more pleasant than the other?

_____

_____

_____

_____

_____

There's Nothing Small About Small Talk

Objective

To practice conversations with a variety of people to increase your comfort in social situations.

What to Know

If you're shy and anxious in social situations, making small talk is an important way to practice your conversational skills.

This worksheet is designed to help you practice small talk with a variety of people. The more often you practice small talk, the more you will be comfortable in other types of social situations. Here are some things to keep in mind when practicing your conversational skills.

- Make eye contact.
- Use open body language.
- Be positive.
- Find things in common to talk about.
- Try using compliments to open a conversation.
- Ask questions, and also state your opinions.
- When you ask a simple question, you might get a one-word answer, so be prepared to ask two or three follow-up questions.
- Give details when you answer questions.
- Pay attention to social cues, such as body language or facial expression, to see whether to continue or stop a conversation.
- Be patient with yourself. If you are shy and find it hard to talk to people, you will need to practice making small talk every day until these conversations become easier.

What to Do

Look for opportunities to start conversations in different situations. Then, use the following table to take notes on these conversations. Record the length of time you spent in each conversation and rate your comfort level from 1 to 10, with 1 is "totally at ease" and 10 is "very uncomfortable." Think of other social situations that might be challenging for you, and write them in the blank spaces.

Assignment	Duration	Comfort Level (1–10)
Start a conversation with a stranger while waiting in line.		
Start a conversation with a relative you don't usually talk to.		
Start a conversation with someone out in public.		
Start a conversation with a stranger about the weather.		
Start up a conversation in a grocery store.		
Start a conversation with a stranger about sports.		
Ask a classmate you don't know very well a question.		
Start a conversation with a server in a restaurant or coffee shop.		
Start a conversation with someone who is walking a dog.		
Ask an older person a question about their past.		
Start a conversation with a classmate you don't know very well.		

Of the conversation challenges, which one was the most difficult for you? Why?

_____

_____

_____

Are You Anxious About Going on Dates?

Objective

To identify the aspects of dating that make you anxious.

What to Know

Dating can be a stressful experience filled with hopes, worries, expectations, and fears. The idea of meeting up with someone you're interested in can be at best worrisome, at worst paralyzing. The list of "what ifs" might make you want to cancel the date! *Will they like me? Will I find them attractive? Will they find me attractive? What will we talk about? What if they see me sweating or blushing? What if I get so nervous I can't even talk? What if we have nothing in common? What if they want to kiss or hug me? What if...?* You get the idea.

What would it be like to relax and enjoy dating—to be present and have fun? Hard to imagine? Well, it can be done.

One technique to overcome your fear of dating is called *exposure therapy*. In this approach, you actually put yourself in the situations you fear in order to overcome your anxiety. It might sound scary at first, but there is a clear method you can follow to become more comfortable with dating.

The first step is to identify the aspects of dating that you fear, and then rate them on a SUDS (subjective units of distress) scale.

What to Do

List at least ten situations that cause anxiety when you think about dating or when you are on a date. (Skip the ratings for now.)

1. _____ SUDS Rating: _____

2. _____ SUDS Rating: _____

3. _____ SUDS Rating: _____

4. _____ SUDS Rating: _____

5. _____ SUDS Rating: _____

6. _____ SUDS Rating: _____

7. _____ SUDS Rating: _____

8. _____ SUDS Rating: _____

9. _____ SUDS Rating: _____

10. _____ SUDS Rating: _____

Now, using the following scale, go back through your list and rate the level of anxiety you feel about each situation.

SUDS Scale*

0   No distress; totally relaxed

1   Alert and awake; concentrating well; no real signs of distress

2   Minimal anxiety/distress

3   Mild anxiety/distress; doesn't interfere with functioning

4   Mild to moderate anxiety/distress; you are more aware of your anxiety

5   Moderate anxiety/distress; uncomfortable, but can continue to function

6   Moderate to strong anxiety/distress; you are aware of your anxiety and how it affects you

7   Quite anxious/distressed; interfering with functioning; physiological signs may be present

8   Very anxious/distressed; can't concentrate; physiological signs are present

9   Extremely anxious/distressed; feeling desperate

10   Highest level of distress/fear/anxiety that you have ever felt

What situation or symptom related to dating causes you the most distress?

_____

_____

_____

*Adapted from Back, S. E., Foa, E. B., Killeen, T. K., Mills, K. L., Teesson, M., Dansky Cotton, B., Carroll, K. M., & Brady, K. T. (2014). *Concurrent treatment of PTSD and substance use disorders using prolonged exposure (COPE): Patient workbook.* Oxford University Press.

Exposure Therapy for Dating Anxiety

Objective

To decrease dating-related anxiety through exposure training.

What to Know

For many teens with social anxiety, dating can cause distress, both before and during the date. Maybe you're worried about making small talk or making a fool of yourself in some way. Maybe you're worried your date will think you're unattractive. Maybe the noise and stimulation is overwhelming. You might believe you have nothing interesting to say. These worries and fears can keep you from participating in many pleasurable things that dating has to offer: caring, sharing, support, romance, friendship, fun, and so on.

You can manage your fears if you're willing to create a plan to gradually face them by doing the very thing you are afraid to do and realizing your worst fears do not come true.

There's no way to go on a test run of a date because any date is a real date! So, exposure therapy for fear of dating begins in a different way from typical exposure therapy. You might first try mock dates with a friend or loved one; then, you might graduate to going on a real date under circumstances that you're less nervous about (for example, if you're worried about eating in front of your date, you might choose to see a movie rather than go out to dinner). The goal is to allow yourself to experience a mild level of anxiety you can learn to cope with—not run away or resort to safety behaviors.

What to Do

You're now ready to go on a mock date. You can set up conditions that might cause you to have similar symptoms as a real situation.

Who can you ask to go on a mock date with you? _____

Let the person know you're trying to *cause* anxiety to flare up. Maybe they can think of ways to throw you off course or challenge you.

Pick a date and time when you would like to schedule your exposure experience.

_____

Pick a specific venue where you'll have your mock date (somewhere public where you might experience social anxiety). Write down your ideas.

_____

_____

What specific mental coping strategies will you try on the mock date?

_____

_____

What specific physical coping strategies will you try on the mock date?

_____

_____

Once you have completed one mock date, schedule as many as you feel are necessary to practice trial dating. Use the following chart to record your mock date experiences. Note the fear you're trying to create. What symptoms arise and how severe are they? What are the habitual anxious thoughts that come up? What would you like to say to yourself instead? Note any reflections.

Fear	Symptom & Severity (0–10)	Physical Strategies Tried	Habitual Thought & Reassuring Statement	Reflections
Losing my train of thought and rambling	*Rapid heartbeat, 5*	*Deep breathing*	*Habitual: They must think I'm an idiot.* *Reassuring: It's okay to lose my train of thought. Everyone does it. Stop, breathe, and refocus.*	*I was very anxious, but I redirected my energy, my breath slowed down, and I was able to refocus.*

If you found this helpful, keep track of your actual dates and record your experiences on the chart or make one of your own. Ask for help from a parent or caregiver, counselor, or friend.

Did you notice any difference between your experience of anxiety symptoms in your practice situations versus a real situation?

_____

_____

_____

More Techniques to Overcome Anxiety

section 3

worksheet

Using a Worry Log

Objective

To record your worries for a two-week period and determine if there are any patterns to your worries.

What to Know

You might spend a lot of time worrying. Are you thinking about the bad things that can happen? Teens with anxiety typically worry not only about big things, but also about little things, such as "Will I forget to submit my paper on time and receive a bad grade?"

Worrying all the time can be a tremendous drain. Are you ready to worry less? Are you ready to have more time for your important relationships, fun activities, schoolwork, and even daily tasks?

The first step to reducing your worrying is to understand it better. You can do this by keeping a worry log, in which you write down the kinds of things you worry about, what triggers you to worry, and how much anxiety your worries cause you.

Consider Tara. She used the worry log for one month and realized how much time she spent worrying about things she had no control over. Her worry log allowed her to realize what caused her to worry, when she usually worried, and how much worrying affected her life. By keeping her worry log, Tara realized that she tended to worry when she was really tired, when she was stressed about school, and when her parents scolded her. She also recognized that her worrying was impacting her grades and she was losing sleep thinking about all the things she was worried about!

What to Do

Make copies of the following chart and record your worries for at least two weeks. Any time you find yourself worrying, write it in the chart. Rate your anxiety from 1 to 10, where 1 is "a little anxiety" and 10 is "the worst anxiety imaginable." Make notes about why you were worried, as well as what triggered your worries.

Date and Time	Why Were You Worried?	What Triggered the Worry?	Level of Anxiety (1–10)

Did you notice any patterns, or was there a particular worry that repeated itself?

_____

_____

_____

Once you became aware that you were worrying, could you stop yourself? If yes, explain how. If no, why not?

_____

_____

_____

Using Humor to Stop Worrying

Objective

To decrease your worrying by distracting yourself with humor.

What to Know

When you have recurring and unwanted thoughts or worries, don't fight them. Instead, embrace them! It may sound strange, but research suggests that the more you try to stop thinking about something, the more you *will* think about it.

Take a moment and give it a try. Close your eyes and visualize an alligator lying on your bed. Think about this image for a minute. Now try *not* to think about an alligator on your bed. If you're like most people, this is very difficult and the image you're trying *not* to think about keeps popping into your mind.

What to Do

What is something you worry about?

_____

_____

Now, take a look at the following humorous ways to deal with worry and put a check mark by things you think you might like to try.

_____ For five minutes, sing a song about your worry to the tune of "Happy Birthday" over and over again.

_____ Draw a funny picture of the worst thing that could happen if what you worry about came true.

_____ Make up a story about your worry, and add a terrible ending.

_____ Write down the worry about 20 times. Then, write it twice more with your non-dominant hand.

_____ Translate your worry into another language (you can use https://translate.google.com). Read the translation aloud five times. Now, do it again in two more languages.

_____ Write down your worry, reversing the letters of each word.

_____ Get a plain T-shirt and write or draw your worry on the shirt with a fabric marker. Make it as colorful as you can, and wear it around the house for a few hours. Don't forget to take a look at yourself in the mirror!

_____ Fill your mouth with food and repeat the thought that worries you five times.

_____ Imagine yourself worrying as if you were in a horror movie. Visualize yourself in the place where you are most likely to worry, except that a similar scary villain is playing you.

_____ Create a comic strip about your worry. If drawing isn't your thing, you can use an app like ToonDraw or Yaya and Zouk: Creation.

_____ Create a rap song about your worries with a program like Smule, AutoRap, or TikTok. Just record your worries, and the app will turn it into a rap song. Play the song at least five times and share it with others.

For one week, try at least one humorous activity every day involving your most significant worry. Rate how you feel before and after each activity from 1 to 10, where 1 is "little or no anxiety" and 10 is "extreme anxiety."

Activity	Date and Time	Anxiety Before (1–10)	Anxiety After (1–10)

As you practiced different activities, did you notice any new thoughts? What were they?

_____

_____

_____

These activities were meant to be humorous. Were they? Did you smile? Did you laugh out loud?

_____

_____

_____

Did you worry less? Why or why not?

_____

_____

_____

Did you share what you were doing with other people? What was their reaction?

_____

_____

_____

Using a Worry Script

Objective

To face and manage your anxious feelings and worries rather than avoid them.

What to Know

You might spend hours each day trying to avoid worrying about things that upset you. Do you distract yourself by checking your phone, playing video games, or even turning to alcohol, drugs, or overeating? None of these things help reduce worrying.

In fact, the harder you try to avoid the thoughts that make you anxious, the worse they get. Trying to push something out of your mind is a little like trying to push a beach ball underwater: It takes a lot of work to keep it down, and the minute you let it go, it pops right back up again.

Rather than putting all your energy into avoiding upsetting thoughts, you can choose to face your fears. Writing worry scripts is one way to help you do this. By writing a worry script about your biggest worry, you'll face your negative thoughts and upsetting feelings rather than avoid them. Writing a script will also help you get a clear picture of what's really upsetting you. Many teens who write a worry script for a few weeks report they feel less anxious about the things they were worrying about.

Here's how to write a worry script:

- Choose a place where you won't be interrupted. Turn off your phone, music, and television. Set aside about 30 minutes to complete each script.
- Write down one thing you're worrying about.
- Write about the worst-case scenario.
- Include vivid details—how things look, sound, and feel. Include your feelings and reactions.
- Write a new script on the *same* subject each day, going deeper into your feelings.
- After about two weeks, you can move to the next worry.

If you feel anxious, or even fearful, while you're writing, keep at it! Experiencing these feelings means you are on the right track. Even though it might be difficult, the more you face your fears and worries, the more likely they will eventually fade.

My Worry Script

Date: _____ Beginning Time: _____ Ending Time: _____

Summarize what you are worrying about in one sentence: _____

_____

_____

Describe your worry in vivid detail:

_____

_____

_____

_____

_____

_____

_____

_____

_____

_____

_____

_____

_____

_____

_____

worksheet

Alter Your Symmetry Rituals

Objective

To decrease your compulsive need for symmetry by changing your usual rituals.

What to Know

Symmetry-driven obsessive-compulsive disorder (OCD) involves the irrational fear or obsession that something terrible will happen if you don't place items or perform acts in a symmetrical and ritualized way. You might feel an overwhelming sense of uneasiness or discomfort when items are not placed in an exact order or in a certain way. For example, you may experience an overwhelming need for items to be balanced, such as holding your phone with evenly placed hands. You may become upset when words or items you believe should be symmetrical don't line up as you think they should.

Interrupting the patterns of symmetry that you feel bound to follow will allow you to increase your awareness of why, when, and how you perform your rituals so you can honestly evaluate your need to continue them.

What to Do

When you are caught up in the OCD cycle of obsessions and compulsions, you may not even realize all the different ritualized behaviors you perform. Preparing a list requires you to acknowledge and accept your actions and recognize the impact they have on your life.

List five symmetry-based rituals you perform.

1. _____

2. _____

3. _____

4. _____

5. _____

Engaging in multiple rituals makes it hard to focus and can keep you from recognizing your obsessive and compulsive patterns. Focusing on one particular ritual encourages you to notice and explore all areas of the behavior you practice, helping you find a way to choose a different approach instead of having your behavior dictated by your fears and obsessions.

Choose one of the five rituals you listed to explore further: _____

Sometimes you'll discover your rituals blend together; you perform them so quickly they become second nature. Taking time to explore your rituals makes it trickier for you to ignore the control they have over you and the impact they have on your life.

What triggers you to perform your ritual?

_____

_____

_____

What outcome are you trying to avoid or escape by performing your ritual?

_____

_____

_____

What are the specific actions you engage in? Are they completed in a certain order or a certain number of times?

_____

_____

_____

Where are you when you are performing this ritual? _____

Is anyone with you when you are performing it, or are you alone? _____

If you sort items, describe any direction that you feel items must face. _____

_____

What is your body doing during the ritual? Are you standing or sitting? Are you holding something? Must your hands be placed in a certain way?

_____

_____

_____

Altering your ritual allows you to become more mindful of the intense effort and time you put into compulsions—time that could be spent doing something you enjoy instead! Making a conscious decision to change your compulsions also helps you reassert your power instead of passively reacting to whatever obsession you are trying to avoid or escape.

Now it's time to change your ritual. Following is a list of ideas, or you can think of your own unique way to alter your ritual.

Suggestions:

- Change the order of the objects you feel compelled to put in a certain way.
  - Example: *Take the items on your desk and put them in different places.*
- Change the order in which you perform the ritual.
  - Example: *If you feel you must dress in a certain order in the morning, change the order of how you get dressed.*
- Change the frequency.
  - Example: *If you have to wash your hands six times, wash them three times instead.*
- Change the amount.
  - Example: *If you always have to have five pencils with you, have three instead.*
- Change how you physically perform your ritual.
  - Example: *If you usually stand, try to sit. If your hands have to be placed exactly on each side of a cup, move them so that one is higher and one is lower. If your eyes are usually closed during your mental ritual, open them.*
- Get creative! Think of your own unique ways to make small or large changes in your rituals.

Now that you've decided what changes you want to make, you're ready to put them in action. Use these steps, and track your progress in the chart that follows.

1. Write down the date, the ritual you chose, and the change you're going to make.
2. Both before and after you change the ritual, rate your anxiety level from 1 to 10, where 1 is "little to no anxiety" and 10 is "very anxious."
3. Keep implementing one or more changes every day for at least a two-week period.
4. When you feel comfortable, try to stop the ritual altogether.
5. As soon you eliminate one ritual, move on to another.

Date	Ritual to Alter	Change(s)	Anxiety Level Before (1–10)	Anxiety Level After (1–10)	Results of Change

Reduce All-or-Nothing Thinking

Objective

To decrease anxiety levels by reducing all-or-nothing thinking.

What to Know

All-or-nothing thinking is a negative thought process and cognitive distortion common in teens with anxiety. When thinking in all-or-nothing terms, your views are often divided in extreme ways. Everything—from your view of yourself to your life experiences—is divided into black-or-white terms. This leaves room for little, if any, gray area in between. Very rarely is anything completely one way or the other. People and situations tend to have varying mixes of negative and positive. For example, even in a bad week, there are usually some good days.

All-or-nothing thinking involves using absolute terms, such as *never* or *always*. You may fail to see the alternatives in a situation or solutions to a problem. If you have anxiety, you might only see the downside to any given situation. You might believe you're either wildly successful or a complete failure.

Here are some tips to correct all-or-nothing thinking:

- Avoid unconditional terms, such as *never*, *always*, or *nothing*.
- Notice when you're thinking in extremes. Ask yourself if there are gray areas.
- Try to find the positive side of a situation or problem.
- When you can only see one side of a situation, seek out advice or support from someone you trust, such as a friend, family member, coach, mentor, counselor, or teacher. They can help you brainstorm solutions and possibilities, allowing you to think beyond absolute terms.

What to Do

The following graphs illustrate that there is a large gray area between the extremes. For each of the categories, circle the number that indicates where you would realistically rate your own experiences.

Your Friends:

1	2	3	4	5	6	7	8	9	10

I have no friends.   Everyone loves me.

School:

1	2	3	4	5	6	7	8	9	10

I will never succeed in school.   I get straight A's without even trying.

Your Family:

1	2	3	4	5	6	7	8	9	10

I feel no support from my family.   My family loves everything I do.

Skills & Talents:

1	2	3	4	5	6	7	8	9	10

I am not skilled in any way.   I do everything perfectly.

What are some ways you can avoid all-or-nothing thinking?

_____

_____

_____

Was it challenging for you to think about different possibilities or solutions? Why?

_____

_____

_____

Who can help you avoid all-or-nothing thinking when you're presented with problems or situations in the future? _____

worksheet

Talk Back to the Thoughts That Make You Anxious

Objective

To talk back to your irrational thoughts with fact-based logic to diminish your anxiety.

What to Know

Irrational thoughts fuel anxiety. Your irrational thoughts (also called *cognitive distortions*) are based on errors in thinking rather than in fact. When you learn to talk back to your irrational thoughts with fact-based logic, you will diminish your anxiety and it will be easier to face your fears.

This worksheet lists irrational thoughts commonly held by teens who experience anxiety. Each statement is followed by a reality-based "talk-back" statement.

What to Do

Begin by reading all the examples carefully, paying particular attention to the talk-back arguments. Notice how they are grounded in fact rather than in fear.

Then, move on to the exercises. Review each of the irrational statements and write in your own rational talk-back statement. (You'll notice the irrational statements are the same as those used in the examples, but your talk-back statements don't have to be exactly the same; they just have to be logical and based on fact. The best talk-back response is the one that works for you!)

Finally, think of any other irrational thoughts you have that fuel your anxiety. Write them down in the blank spaces at the end, then write a talk-back statement for each.

Examples:

1. My anxiety will cause me to have a heart attack.

   Talk Back: Anxiety can simulate symptoms of a heart attack, but these symptoms are not dangerous and will soon pass. I don't have to be afraid.

2. If I am in a crowd, I will faint.

   Talk Back: If I feel light-headed or dizzy, I can just breathe deeply and slowly to get more oxygen. I've never fainted in a crowd before. I'm not going to faint.

3. I feel like I am going crazy.

   Talk Back: Anxiety can play tricks on my mind, but these thoughts and feelings will soon pass. Being afraid doesn't mean I am going crazy.

4. People will think I'm weird because I'm so anxious about everything.

   Talk Back: Lots of people have anxiety. Everyone knows what it feels like to be anxious. People won't think I am weird.

5. People will think less of me because I'm so anxious.

   Talk Back: Most people don't judge others harshly. If someone doesn't like something about me, it won't negatively affect me.

6. I will do something inappropriate and people will think I'm crazy, or I could even get into trouble.

   Talk Back: The fear of doing something inappropriate is just a thought I'm having now. I've never done anything like this before, and I never will! People won't think I'm crazy, and I won't get into trouble.

7. Something terrible will happen if I _____.

   Talk Back: This is an example of catastrophic thinking. It's a symptom of anxiety and not reality based. The probability of this happening is almost non-existent. I don't need to avoid this situation.

8. If I feel really anxious, I must leave the room.

   Talk Back: I don't have to leave the room if I'm uncomfortable. I know these feelings will soon pass, and I can just let them go.

9. I can't let anyone find out I have problems with anxiety; I must keep this a secret.

   Talk Back: Many people are anxious. Hiding my problems doesn't help. Facing my fears is the only way to get rid of them for good. Telling people about my problems could help relieve my anxiety.

10. If I have an anxiety attack while at _____, I will be so embarrassed!

    Talk Back: The nature of my anxiety is that I fear things that aren't true. There's no shame in having a problem with anxiety. I won't be embarrassed if I have a panic attack. I will breathe deeply and calm myself down.

11. I will always be anxious.

    Talk Back: I can develop skills to face my fears and get rid of my anxiety forever.

12. I can't _____ because of my anxiety.

    Talk Back: I can do it. I'm not going to give into my fears and restrict my life.

Exercises:

1. My anxiety will cause me to have a heart attack.

   Talk Back: _____

   _____

2. If I'm in a crowd, I will faint.

   Talk Back: _____

   _____

3. I feel like I am going crazy.

   Talk Back: _____

   _____

4. People will think I'm weird because I'm so anxious about everything.

   Talk Back: _____

   _____

5. People will think less of me because I'm so anxious.

   Talk Back: _____

   _____

6. I will do something inappropriate and people will think I'm crazy, or I could even get into trouble.

   Talk Back: _____

   _____

7. Something terrible will happen if I _____.

   Talk Back: _____

   _____

8. If I feel really anxious, I must leave the room.

   Talk Back: _____

   _____

9. I can't let anyone find out I have problems with anxiety; I must keep this a secret.

   Talk Back: _____

   _____

10. If I have an anxiety attack while at _____, I will be so embarrassed!

    Talk Back: _____

    _____

11. I will always have problems with anxiety.

    Talk Back: _____

    _____

12. I can't _____ because of my anxiety.

    Talk Back: _____

    _____

13. Irrational fear-based thought:

    _____

    Talk Back: _____

    _____

14. Irrational fear-based thought:

    _____

    Talk Back: _____

    _____

15. Irrational fear-based thought:

    _____

    Talk Back: _____

    _____

16. Irrational fear-based thought:

    _____

    Talk Back: _____

    _____

17. Irrational fear-based thought:

    _____

    Talk Back: _____

    _____

How Do You View Yourself?

Objective

To develop a positive but realistic self-image to reduce your anxiety.

What to Know

Sometimes teens have a poor self-image and dwell on their faults rather than their strengths, increasing their anxiety. They measure themselves against an unrealistic ideal of the way they "should" be. Where does that unrealistic ideal come from? Teens who grew up in families where there was a high demand for perfection or achievement sometimes struggle to fulfill those expectations in their academic and home lives. Other teens might be criticized for the least little flaw and focus on those flaws as core parts of their self-image—not learning that, in fact, nobody's perfect. If they do 99 out of 100 things right, they'll dwell on the one "wrong" thing and worry about how they can "fix" themselves.

Does this sound familiar? Do you have a running narrative in your mind about how you're failing to live up to your own or someone else's standards? Do you criticize yourself or feel like you're not good enough? What would it be like to embrace yourself fully, warts and all?

What to Do

The following list provides some ways you can improve your self-image. Write down your thoughts and goals in response to each prompt.

1. **Challenge your negative thoughts.** Listen closely to what your inner critic says. Ask yourself, "Is that actually true?" Challenge those ingrained beliefs that bring down your self-esteem. Write some statements to counter them here. Example: Instead of "I'm not good enough," try "I'm a worthy and capable human being with strengths and weaknesses."

   _____

   _____

   _____

   _____

2. **Develop a kind inner voice.** When you hear your inner critical voice, imagine that you're listening to people you care about. What would you want to say to help them feel better about themselves? Use those words and that kind tone with yourself too, and keep practicing making that shift for as long as you need.

_____

_____

_____

_____

3. **Celebrate your accomplishments and strengths.** Teens with a poor self-image often focus too much on what they haven't done or accomplished versus what they have. Write all the accomplishments you can think of, even from when you were little. They can be big, small, public, or private. Then write down your strengths, such as reliability, caring, curiosity, or strength. Use extra paper if you need to. Go for it!

_____

_____

_____

_____

4. **Avoid "compare despair."** Do you find yourself comparing yourself to your peers? It's easy to feel down about yourself if you're always comparing yourself to others. This happens a lot on social media, where other teens always *seem* to have everything you want—whether it's relationships, perfect grades, nice clothes, or success. Remember, those posts are just a selected reality, not real life itself. Refocus on your own strengths and work on not measuring yourself against others. What are a few specific steps you can take to spend less time comparing yourself to others and remind yourself of your own strengths?

_____

_____

_____

_____

5. **Notice what's in your control and what isn't.** If your anxiety is related to things you can't control ("If only I were taller, I'd be happier," "If only I looked like _____, I'd be popular," etc.), then you are setting yourself up for continued misery. Focus your energy on identifying things in your life that you can do something about, and begin to act on those. Write them here.

_____

_____

_____

_____

6. **Do something you love to do!** Are you passionate about cooking? Reading? Fashion? Singing? Sports? Computers? Animals? What are you currently doing or not doing to invest time and energy into your passions? What would you like to do more of? Note any excuses or rationalizations you might think of that keep you from pursuing these activities.

_____

_____

_____

_____

7. **Be grateful.** Establishing a "gratitude practice" every day can help boost your mood and your self-esteem. List here some things you appreciate. They can be small, like the pleasure of chewing a tasty piece of cheese, or big, like your health or your family or having a warm bed at night.

_____

_____

_____

_____

8. **Give back/pay it forward.** If you're anxious, it's often hard to think about anything but your worries. You might have trouble seeing other people's needs sometimes. Consider volunteering some time to a cause that has meaning for you, such as a food bank or an animal shelter. You might also consider what skills and talents you have that you could pass along to someone else. You could be a mentor or tutor to a younger child or a volunteer who helps others to discover their own strengths. What goes around comes around, as they say. Studies show that the happiest people are the ones who are involved in serving others. Write down some ideas for how and where you could donate your time.

_____

_____

_____

_____

9. **Find positive people in your life.** Maybe you feel down a lot and avoid hanging out with others whose lives might seem "better" than yours. Identify the people in your life whom you feel comfortable with, who bolster your self-esteem, and who see your wonderful qualities and accept your flaws and mistakes. Make an effort to spend more time with them and less time with people who bring you down. What would you like to do to meet that goal?

_____

_____

_____

_____

10. **Exercise!** Sure, you've probably heard this a million times, but it's true. Exercise has been proven to lessen anxiety and help you feel better about yourself. Releasing positive hormones such as endorphins can be a great side effect of increased movement. Set small, realistic goals (e.g., walking for a few minutes a day) and build up to more if you wish. Write your specific exercise goals here. Then, as they say, just do it!

_____

_____

_____

_____

11. **Step out of your bubble.** Are you stuck in a routine? Do you feel like a stick-in-the-mud as a result? Make a plan to do something different, whether it's visiting a place you've never been, reconnecting with an old friend, or going to an event where you are likely to meet new people. It can feel challenging at first, but moving out of your comfort zone can give you a boost of energy and a new perspective on the possibilities for your life. Write your bubble-busting plan here.

_____

_____

_____

_____

What was it like to reflect on the previous suggestions? Which ones do you feel excited about? Which ones do you feel some resistance to?

_____

_____

_____

_____

For those suggestions to which you feel some resistance, what encouraging words would you like to offer that part of yourself in order to boost your motivation?

_____

_____

_____

_____

Who in your life loves you unconditionally? Make a plan to connect with this person regularly to remind yourself of your worth and your positive qualities. Then, remember to tell yourself the things this person tells you. How does this person feel about you?

_____

_____

_____

_____

worksheet

It's Okay if You're Not Perfect!

Objective

To deliberately do something considered socially inappropriate and tolerate the discomfort this action causes.

What to Know

You might think that in order to be successful in life, you need to perform at the highest level possible—whether that's in school, in your extracurricular activities, at work, or even with your friends and family. It's reasonable for you to have high standards and work hard to meet your goals. Unfortunately, disciplined behavior can cross the line to perfectionism if it interferes with your social, emotional, or academic functioning. Striving to be perfect can actually stop you from reaching your goals.

Perfectionism is fueled by, and fuels, anxiety. You might struggle daily with worry, anxiety, and an intense fear of failure. Anxious thoughts support perfectionistic behaviors, and when your results fall short of expectations, you probably experience even greater anxiety. It can be a hard cycle to break.

Consider Heather. At a choral concert, 60 choir members walked up to the stage on a set of steps visible to the nearly 2,500 people on the expansive lawn at an outdoor venue. Heather, who has a fear of making a fool of herself in public, stumbled on one of the steps and fell— *splat*—bracing herself with her hands. People helped her up, and she took her place in the lineup, but she was mortified. She was sure everyone in the choir and in the audience was laughing at her and thinking she was a "clumsy idiot." She felt like she had failed, and she had a difficult time focusing throughout the event because she was beating herself up. It's likely that Heather was the only one who even gave any thought to it after it happened, much less a critical thought. People probably felt empathy and hoped she was okay.

What if you were to experience yourself as imperfect by embarrassing yourself *on purpose*? You might feel anxious at the thought! This form of exposure therapy is called *constructive embarrassment*. The idea is to expose yourself to uncomfortable feelings and learn to tolerate them—to actually welcome the feeling of embarrassment or humiliation so you can get used to it and realize that nothing catastrophic will happen and you're human, just like everyone else!

What to Do

Check any of the following statements that apply to you:

_____ I'm dissatisfied with a standard that others view as acceptable.

_____ I often procrastinate until I'm sure of what to do and/or how to earn a high grade on an assignment.

_____ I'm afraid to answer questions in class for fear of being wrong.

_____ I'm afraid to take risks.

_____ I'm angry with myself, and say harsh things to myself, when I make a mistake.

_____ I avoid starting tasks because I'm afraid I won't do them "right" or "well."

_____ I get very upset when my grades are lower than I expect.

_____ I can't cope with mistakes.

_____ I feel like I've failed if I don't say and do things perfectly.

_____ I take criticism personally.

_____ I do my work or complete tests slowly to avoid mistakes.

_____ I focus on neatness and the appearance of my work.

_____ I start over repeatedly to "get it right."

Total checked statements: _____

If you checked five or more statements, you probably try very hard to be perfect, leading to worry and anxiety.

This exercise instructs you to plan a few "socially inappropriate" things to do in public. The following list has some possible activities. Feel free to add your own situations to the list. On each line, rate the anxiety that each activity would cause you using a scale of 1 to 10, where 1 is "little to no anxiety" and 10 is "extreme distress."

_____ As you're walking down the hall at school, stumble and fall on purpose.

_____ Go to a movie after it has already started and ask to climb over people.

_____ Intentionally misspell a word in a message or social media post.

_____ Make a phone call; then, say you have the wrong number and hang up.

_____ Spill your drink or drop a tray of food in the cafeteria.

_____ Dress casually for a formal event (or vice versa).

_____ Talk to yourself out loud in class.

_____ Face the wrong way in an elevator.

_____ Hum softly during class.

_____ Go to school and walk around with a speck of food on your face.

_____ Wear mismatched socks or shoes.

_____ Ask a question in class that you're worried might make you appear stupid.

_____ Intentionally answer questions incorrectly on a test.

_____ Skip instead of walk down the street.

_____ Pause for ten seconds while giving a presentation.

_____ Order a messy meal when you are on a date.

_____ Your own idea: _____

_____ Your own idea: _____

_____ Your own idea: _____

Now you'll practice doing the activities in public. Choose the activities you marked 1 or 2 first, then work up to trying a 5 or 6. You might want to invite a friend or group of friends to join you as you practice the skills. Then, record your reflections about the experience.

"Socially inappropriate" activities you did:

_____

_____

_____

_____

Describe in detail your experience engaging in these "socially inappropriate" activities.

_____

_____

_____

_____

What is the worst thing that happened during any of these activities? Did anyone make comments or look at you in a strange way?

_____

_____

_____

_____

What thoughts did you have after you completed this exercise? Do you feel less anxious about the possibility of being imperfect?

_____

_____

_____

_____

Practicing doing the things you fear most is considered to be the best way to overcome your perfectionism. Do you think you can continue this practice? Why or why not?

_____

_____

_____

_____

Face Your Fears with Acceptance and Commitment Therapy

Objective

To face and manage your fears instead of avoiding them.

What to Know

You might feel that paralyzing fear consumes and shapes your life, like a vicious circle or trap from which you can't escape. It's often the most difficult aspect of anxiety to overcome. You fear your own mind, which is filled with unwelcome and disturbing thoughts. You fear losing control of yourself and saying or doing things that are totally against your values.

Imagine you did something different, something that on the surface seems ridiculous—crazy, even! What if instead of trying to control your reaction to a frightening image that you can't unsee or avoid a terrible thought, you become aware of your fears, face them, speak about them aloud, and accept them as something that makes you human? What if you acknowledge your difficulties and the role fear has played in your life? What if you embrace your perceived weaknesses, while also acknowledging your strength and resilience?

Your natural tendency when faced with overwhelming fear might be to fight it by trying to control it. However, this approach only serves to increase anxiety, as the fear only temporarily subsides.

Drawing upon the teachings of mindfulness, acceptance and commitment therapy (ACT) recognizes that suffering stems from the tendency to escape or avoid pain instead of facing it. You disconnect from the present and attach to negative thoughts that you mistakenly think define you. This dissatisfaction is intensified when you base your actions on those fears instead of acting based on your values.

One of the major principles of ACT is to accept your reactions and be present with them, no matter how disturbing they are. Practicing acceptance may at first make you feel very anxious, but being able to tolerate your anxious feelings by fully experiencing the sensations, thoughts, and emotions that accompany your fears is the first step toward decreasing the power your fears have over you.

What to Do

Place a check by the fears that dominate your life, and add any fears you have that are not listed here.

_____ Being disappointed	_____ Being hurt
_____ Feeling embarrassed	_____ Feeling like a failure
_____ Feeling anxious	_____ Becoming dependent
_____ Being different	_____ Appearing crazy
_____ Being uncomfortable	_____ Being lonely
_____ Making a decision	_____ Making a mistake
_____ Being misunderstood	_____ Hurting others
_____ Losing control	_____ Being imperfect
_____ Experiencing pain	_____ Feeling rejected
_____ Seeming stupid	_____ Facing the unknown
_____ Other: _____	_____ Other: _____

Choose at least three fears from your list and, using the prompts that follow, write about how they have impacted your life. As you write, take these steps:

- Observe what you're experiencing without reacting.
- Let your emotions or thoughts happen without giving in to your fears.
- Recognize the difficulty that experiencing these fears has made in your life without judging or criticizing yourself.
- Give yourself permission to be fearful.

My fear of _____ has stopped me from going to the following places I would like to go:

_____

My fear of _____ has made me afraid to try the following things:

_____

My fear of _____ has caused me so much anxiety that I have resorted to the following activities in order to reduce my anxiety:

_____

My fear of _____ has impacted my relationships in the following ways:

_____

My fear of _____ has influenced my plans for the future by:

_____

My fear of _____ has impacted my life by:

_____

How well were you able to observe and not react to your fears and anxiety?

_____

_____

_____

How well were you able to allow your emotions or thoughts to happen without reacting?

_____

_____

_____

What do you think will happen if you give yourself permission to be fearful?

_____

_____

_____

What to Do When You Worry Too Much About Your Health

Objective

To reduce your excessive worrying about your health by learning different strategies for managing your anxious thoughts and feelings.

What to Know

You've probably seen characters on TV and in movies who are considered hypochondriacs: people who worry excessively about their health and who interpret any ache or pain as a sign of a serious illness.

But worrying about your health all the time is no laughing matter. This type of worrying can be part of an anxiety disorder and, paradoxically, worrying about your health can actually cause physical symptoms that can make you feel worse and cause more worry. You might constantly seek reassurance that you're not dying of a fatal disease, but often reassurance doesn't diminish the worry. If you constantly worry that you're sick, you might think that your parents, and even your doctors, are missing something, which creates more stress. This can become a vicious cycle.

Chronic worrying about your health, and even about your death, is just a flow of thoughts and, in reality, has no special power over you. In this worksheet, you'll explore different strategies to overcome your health anxiety.

What to Do

Review the following list and put a check next to the items that apply to you.

_____ I worry that any physical symptoms or sensations are a sign that I have an illness.

_____ My parents or caregivers frequently take me to see doctors to seek reassurance that my symptoms are not serious, only to be told that either nothing is wrong or that the problem is not serious.

_____ I use the internet to research my physical symptoms.

_____ I constantly check my body, wondering if something is wrong.

_____ I seek my parents', friends', or others' validation or reassurance about my health.

_____ I avoid going out for fear of catching an illness or being exposed to germs or toxins.

_____ I don't tell anyone about my worries because people tend to laugh at me or downplay my concerns, which makes me feel even more anxious and alone.

Describe your experiences:

_____

_____

_____

When did you first start worrying about your health? _____

Do you have a family history of people with anxiety about health or physical concerns? _____

How might your family history or the messages you heard when you were little support your worries?

_____

_____

_____

What are the consequences of your chronic worries about your health (for example, avoiding people, irritating people, missing school, failing to fulfill your goals)?

_____

_____

_____

Describe your level of motivation to make changes regarding your health anxiety, where 0 is "not motivated," 1 is "somewhat motivated," 2 is "moderately motivated," and 3 is "highly motivated": _____

If you wrote a 0 or 1, what can help you become more motivated to change?

_____

_____

_____

The following is a list of steps to reduce worries about your health. If you find that your ability to participate in normal daily activities is seriously affected by your health worries, please talk to a trusted adult, such as a parent or caregiver, guidance counselor, or therapist.

1. **Schedule a medical exam.** Schedule a complete physical to properly assess your current health and rule out medical reasons for any symptoms you're experiencing.

2. **Educate yourself about physical symptoms.** Learn that certain bodily sensations that you think are dangerous or fatal are not necessarily indications of an underlying illness. For instance, there can be many explanations for headaches; it's seldom a sign of a brain tumor.

3. **Avoid the internet.** A minor symptom, such as a headache or stomachache, can yield scary results, such as tumors or cancers, which worsen anxiety. If you do this habitually, you might consider setting a goal of cutting back and eventually eliminating your searches.

4. **Stop checking yourself.** Stop taking your temperature, measuring your blood pressure, or taking your pulse. Find something outside of yourself and your body to focus on.

5. **Give away or dispose of any medical devices that are not doctor prescribed.**

6. **Find a support group of teens who share similar worries.** Exchange information and coping strategies in order to feel less alone.

7. **Exercise.** Moving your body can help you manage stress, depression, and anxiety. You can keep it simple, such as a short walk or run, a bike ride, or a visit to the gym. Or you can do something more active, such as rowing, swimming, hiking, or mountain climbing. Your overall health can improve as a result of regular exercise, and you can begin to feel better about yourself.

8. **Practice telling yourself you're fine and you're causing yourself undue stress.**

9. **Meditate or practice deep breathing.** This will calm your body down.

10. **Examine the evidence for your fear.** Is it actually true? Might there be another way to look at the symptom? Treat your thoughts and worries as a habit that is keeping you from having a pleasant day or a pleasant life. This takes time and consistent practice, so be patient.

Which of these strategies are you willing to try?

_____

_____

_____

Whom can you ask for help with your health worries?

_____

Using Visual Metaphors to Accept Your Worries and Distressing Thoughts

Objective

To use visual metaphors to detach from your worries and distressing thoughts to reduce your anxiety.

What to Know

You might spend a lot of time and energy trying to get rid of your upsetting thoughts and worries. What if you stop trying to get rid of them at all? This may seem strange because it's the opposite of what you feel like doing, but the more you try to get rid of your thoughts, the harder it is to get rid of them! When you learn to accept your thoughts and detach from them, they will no longer have power over you.

Stop struggling with your worries! Just accept them. Don't try to distract yourself. Don't try to change your thoughts. Certainly, don't try to dull your thoughts with drugs or alcohol. Also, don't pretend your anxieties and worries don't exist.

Instead, as difficult as this sounds, just accept your worries, detach from them, and observe them without reacting to them in an emotional way. Try to "objectify" your worries, remembering that your thoughts are just thoughts—they have no special powers.

What to Do

This worksheet includes four metaphors that can help you understand and practice the principle of detaching from your worries by objectifying your thoughts and just observing them. Read the different metaphors and observe whether they help you feel less anxious. Then, complete the activity and questions that follow.

1. **Don't struggle in quicksand.** When you struggle to get out of quicksand, you sink deeper. When you relax and float, you will eventually find you're able to swim or walk out of the quicksand. Contrary to popular movies, quicksand does not "suck you down." Quicksand is usually shallow and, when you stop struggling, it's easy to get out.

   Try using this metaphor to stop resisting your worries. Imagine your worries are a pool of quicksand. Struggling will make it harder for you to get out. Accepting your worries as just thoughts and not real dangers will rob them of their power. When you stop struggling, your worries lose their power over you. Just walk away.

2. **Ignore annoying passengers in your car.** You've probably had the experience of riding in a car with annoying passengers. Maybe a complaining friend is sitting next to you, or your siblings are making a lot of noise. So, what do you do? You just consciously tune out the noise from the passengers in the car and let it fade into the background. You're aware of the annoyance, but you tune it out.

   Now, sit back and visualize yourself riding in a car, but your worries are the passengers. They are clamoring to get your attention, but you just tune them out. They are just background noise as you keep on going about your daily routine.

3. **Watching the worry train.** Imagine your worries are cars on a train. Each car contains a different worry. Visualize each car on the train and think for a moment about the worry that's in each one. Now, sit back and visualize this train pulling out of the station. Watch it as it rounds the bend and then continues on a journey out of sight, taking your worries away.

4. **Clouds floating by.** Think about something that you're worried about. Say this worry out loud and visualize the worst thing that could happen. Now, take a photo in your mind of that worry. Imagine that photo is resting on a cloud. Don't do anything to make the cloud go away, but just let it float away on its own, carrying off the picture of your worry. Watch it from the ground and see what happens to it.

   Now, practice using these metaphors every day for two weeks. Even if you're not worrying at the time, you should still complete the practice. Use the following chart to record your experience. In the columns that ask you to rate your anxiety level before, during, and after completing the exercise, use a scale of 1 to 10, where 1 is "very calm and disengaged from your worries" and 10 is "very anxious." In the Notes column, reflect on your experience.

Date	Visual Metaphor You Used	How Did You Feel Before? (1–10)	How Did You Feel During? (1–10)	How Did You Feel After? (1–10)	Notes

Describe how you felt before and after the visualization exercises. Did you notice that you felt less anxious or worried after each exercise?

_____

_____

_____

Describe any changes you noticed in your moods or distressing feelings over these two weeks.

_____

_____

_____

What other changes did you notice (thoughts, behaviors, reactions, feelings, and so forth)?

_____

_____

_____

Controlling Your Hair Pulling

Objective

To control compulsive hair pulling by using behavioral techniques to reduce or eliminate the behavior.

What to Know

Trichotillomania (pronounced TRICK-uh-TILL-uh-MAIN-ee-uh), abbreviated as TTM, is also called *hair-pulling disorder*. It's a psychological problem that involves recurrent, irresistible urges to pull out hair from your scalp, eyebrows, or other areas of your body, despite trying to stop.

TTM can be related to both negative and positive emotions. On the one hand, hair pulling is a way to deal with stress, anxiety, tension, boredom, loneliness, fatigue, or frustration. On the other hand, you might find that it feels good, so you continue the behavior in order to evoke that positive feeling.

You can learn skills to manage your hair pulling, including a strategy called *habit reversal training*. This involves developing an awareness of the thoughts, feelings, and situations that occur before and after your hair pulling (your triggers) and then using relaxation techniques and competing response training to stop your hair pulling.

Note: *The basic principles of habit reversal training are explained in this worksheet, but this approach is best done in collaboration with a trained therapist.*

What to Do

What are the negative consequences of hair pulling for you?

_____

_____

_____

What would you like to gain from trying to control your hair-pulling behaviors?

_____

_____

_____

Describe your level of motivation to reduce or stop your hair pulling, where 0 is "not motivated," 1 is "slightly motivated," 2 is "moderately motivated," and 3 is "highly motivated": _____

Habit Reversal Training

Drs. Nathan Azrin and Gregory Nunn developed behavioral approaches, including habit reversal training (HRT), to deal with hair pulling. The four primary components of HRT are:

1. **Self-awareness training.** Keep a detailed record of all instances when you pull out your hair, including when, where, why, and with whom this happens. Note all urges and sensations associated with the hair pulling before, during, and after it occurs.

2. **Relaxation training.** Practice progressive muscle relaxation exercises or other body-focused relaxation techniques, such as a body scan.

3. **Diaphragmatic breathing.** Learn this deep breathing skill, which can relax the mind and body.

4. **Competing response training.** Learn a muscle tensing action that competes with the hair-pulling behavior. For instance, a competing response would be the opposite of the repetitive behavior and something that you can do for more than two or three minutes. Some experts suggest balling up your hands into a fist and holding them rigidly on the side of your body, or you can tense your arm muscles over and over, tensing and releasing, until the urge subsides or disappears.

Keep track of when you use your HRT strategies. Notice in particular any urges and attempts to use a competing response so you can see improvement over time.

Circumstances: When, Where, with Whom	Why Did You Pull Your Hair?	My Emotions Before Pulling	My Emotions During Pulling	HRT Strategy Used	My Emotions After Using the Strategy

worksheet

Stop Yourself from Fainting When You Get a Shot or Have Blood Drawn

Objective

To use the applied tension technique when you are getting an injection or blood draw to avoid fainting.

What to Know

Nobody really likes getting an injection or having blood drawn. Most teens feel a little nervous, even queasy, before going to an appointment when they expect these medical procedures to occur. However, some teens have a reaction that goes well beyond being nervous. If you start to sweat, hyperventilate, feel dizzy, or even faint every time you even think about needles, then you may be one of tens of thousands of people who suffer from blood/injection/injury phobia.

Fainting is caused by a sudden drop in your heart rate or blood pressure. Most of the time when you're anxious or fearful, your heart rate and blood pressure actually go up. This is why it's so rare to faint when you're feeling anxious. However, some people with a fear of blood or needles experience an initial increase and then a sudden drop in their blood pressure, which can result in fainting. For many teens, the fear of fainting overrides the fear of needles and blood. In the worst-case scenario, you might avoid getting necessary medical procedures because of your fears.

If you do have a fear of fainting, you should know that injuries caused by fainting are actually pretty rare. However, it's important to tell any medical professional you are seeing that this is a concern of yours, particularly if you've fainted before or are currently feeling light-headed. Then they can take extra precautions, such as having you lie down or drink some juice, to help prevent you from fainting or from being injured if you do.

There is also something that you can do all on your own to help you avoid fainting: a technique called *applied tension*. This worksheet shows you how to master the applied tension technique, which is easy to learn (although it takes a little practice).

122

What to Do

Note: *You'll need to practice the exercise for at least a week prior to getting an injection or blood draw.*

Sit in a comfortable chair for this exercise. First, tense the muscles in your arms, legs, and torso for about 20 to 30 seconds. You'll know you're doing it correctly if your face gets warm as you tense up. Then, relax your body for 20 to 30 seconds. Repeat this four to five times. Note that the goal is not to become completely relaxed, as this will cause your blood pressure to drop. Rather, the goal is to let your body return to a normal state (not overly tense or completely relaxed).

Practice this technique four to five times a day for at least a week before the day that you're scheduled to get an injection or blood draw. It's important to practice so you feel comfortable with the technique before having to use it. Use the following chart to track your practice. Each time you practice, think about why you are anxious about getting an injection/blood draw (for example, you might remember a time you had a problem getting an injection or blood draw). Rate your anxiety on a scale of 1 to 10, where 1 is "no anxiety or fear" and 10 is "so anxious you feel faint."

Once you have practiced the technique for at least a week, it will be easy to do if you find yourself feeling light-headed during the injection or blood draw. You can do the exercise while the procedure is going on, but don't tense the arm that is receiving the needle, since this will make it more painful. Instead, relax the arm with the needle while tensing the other parts of your body.

Date of scheduled medical visit: _____

Date	Time	Number of Repetitions (Tensed, Relaxed)	Rate Your Fear/ Anxiety Level (1–10)

worksheet

Curb Your Compulsions to Diminish Your Anxiety

Objective

To decrease your anxiety and regain power over compulsions by purposely shortening the length of your compulsive behavior.

What to Know

As you know, engaging in compulsions can be incredibly time consuming, essentially stealing precious moments of time that you could be spending with your family and friends or participating in an activity you enjoy. If you experience compulsions frequently, you might repeat your compulsive behavior past the point of exhaustion, and yet you still are unable to stop.

Do you often feel as though you are being held hostage by your compulsions after losing countless hours conducting a ritual over and over again, washing your hands incessantly, or checking each and every light in your house only to wonder "what if?" and find yourself checking all over again? Do you ever look at the clock in shock at the realization of how much time you have wasted?

What to Do

This worksheet will help you shorten the length of time you spend on your compulsions and establish control over how your time is spent. This exercise gives you permission to feel your anxiety, while simultaneously allowing you to recognize you're the one giving yourself permission to indulge in your compulsion; therefore, you also have the power to end it when you feel the time is right.

Fill in the following compulsion log for one week. Note how often and for how long you engage in your compulsions. Then, when you find yourself engaging in a compulsive behavior, set a timer for a period that's at least *ten minutes less* than the time you usually engage in this compulsion. You might also have a friend or family member remind you when it's time to end.

In the columns that ask you to rate your anxiety level, use a scale of 1 to 10, where 1 is "very calm/little to no anxiety" and 10 is "very anxious."

Make a copy of the chart and continue the exercise for consecutive two-week intervals, lessening the time spent on the compulsion by an additional ten minutes until you eventually stop engaging in the behavior.

	Obsession	Compulsive Behavior	Anxiety Associated with the Compulsion (1–10)	Time Spent Engaging in the Compulsion	Goal Time (At least 10 minutes less)	Anxiety Associated with the Reduced Time (1–10)
Example	*Boyfriend is ignoring me*	*Checking social media*	*8*	*2 hours*	*90 minutes*	*7*
Day 1						
Day 2						
Day 3						
Day 4						
Day 5						
Day 6						
Day 7						

How did facing your compulsions instead of fighting against them impact your level of anxiety?

_____

_____

_____

How successful were you in decreasing the time you spend on your compulsions? Were you able to stop any of your compulsive behaviors entirely? Explain.

_____

_____

_____

Reduce Overstimulation to Focus on Yourself

Objective

To relax your mind and body by identifying and limiting the activities in your life that cause anxiety and keep your mind on "alert."

What to Know

You probably live in a world full of stimulation: TV, radio, music, smartphones, computers, video games, traffic, and other noises. Sometimes it's out of your control, but other times you seek out the stimulation—perhaps to avoid feelings, or perhaps because silence feels weird or uncomfortable.

Constant stimulation and mental activity can lead to anxiety, attention and memory problems, and difficulty concentrating or focusing. All of this can be challenging and stressful.

Give your brain a break. That doesn't mean you need to go off to a Zen retreat and take a vow of silence. You can experiment with simple ways to take breaks from all the noise and stimulation. Start by noticing that there's a quiet place deep inside of you—if only you take a moment to listen.

What to Do

Here is a list of things that might keep you from relaxing your mind. For the next week, select several items from this list and cut back these habits or revise your schedule, if possible. See if you notice any change in your feelings or general mood.

- Checking email
- Checking social media accounts
- Going out with friends
- Visiting friends and family
- Going to loud outdoor concerts
- Going to parties
- Listening to music
- Responding to texts
- Talking on the phone
- Watching streaming videos

What else would you add to this list? _____

What are the top three items that are getting in the way of relaxing your mind?

1. _____

2. _____

3. _____

On a scale of 1 to 10, where 1 is "very unwilling," 5 is "somewhat willing," and 10 is "very willing," how willing are you to experiment with cutting back on or eliminating your top three activities for the next week? _____

If you want to cut back, when and how much will you allow yourself to do this activity? For example, "Check Snapchat only three times a day for no more than five minutes." Be very specific.

_____

_____

_____

_____

_____

_____

Tell someone you trust about your choice and ask for accountability. Better yet, find an "unplugging" buddy!

Name of person/buddy: _____

How do you feel about cutting back on or eliminating the activities that interfere with relaxing your mind?

_____

_____

_____

Use the following chart to keep track of your progress. Each day, cut back or eliminate an activity, and note for how long you did the activity. Finally, reflect on your thoughts and feelings about cutting out the activity.

Date	Activity You Cut Back or Eliminated	How Long?	Thoughts	Feelings

What was it like to cut back or eliminate activities that cause anxiety and keep your mind on alert?

_____

_____

_____

Did this exercise reduce your anxiety and/or help you relax? How so?

_____

_____

_____

Mindful Meditation 101

Objective

To quiet your mind and body through practicing formal and informal mindful meditation.

What to Know

Mindfulness means noticing what's happening right here and now, without judgment and with acceptance. Even a few minutes of quieting the mind and body on a regular basis can reap big benefits: less anxiety and stress, and improvements in memory and attention. You're training your brain to default to a more relaxed state. That happens only with regular practice. Just as you wouldn't expect a marathon runner to be able to run a race without training, don't expect that you'll immediately reap the benefits of meditation. Go slow and steady, one step at a time.

You can find meditation, mindfulness, or guided visualization recordings on YouTube, in meditation apps, as podcasts, and so on. Sometimes you might want to meditate with music, sometimes without. Explore, experiment, and find what works best for you.

There are two categories of mindfulness meditation practices: formal and informal. *Formal practice* requires setting aside a specific time each day (or multiple times a day) to be mindful, and it can be done either sitting or walking. *Informal practice* refers to paying mindful, nonjudgmental attention while doing certain routine daily activities, such as taking a shower, washing the dishes, making your bed, going for a walk, and so on. Start by choosing one daily activity at a time so you don't get overwhelmed.

What to Do

In this exercise, you'll start with the formal practice of sitting meditation. Sitting meditation requires setting aside a specific time each day, twice a day, or as often as you can to sit quietly with your eyes closed (or open, gazing steadily downward, if you prefer). Experts often recommend twenty minutes per day, but if that doesn't work for you, try starting with ten, or five, or even three minutes. You can always build up over time, just like marathon runners in training.

For your sitting meditation, find a time when you can eliminate all distractions and unplug from the world. To start, you might choose to repeat a mantra, which is a word of your choice (such as *peace*, *calm*, *one*, or *love*) that you can use as your anchor when your mind wanders—which it inevitably will.

Don't worry, and don't judge yourself. Just watch the thoughts floating past you, like clouds in the sky. *The mindful moment comes when you notice your mind wandering.* Simply bring your attention back to your anchor. You can also use your breath as an anchor or any mindful self-compassion phrases. By regularly practicing sitting still and simply noticing the flow of thoughts and sensations without judgment and with acceptance, you'll get better at noticing when you are not mindful. Again, that "waking-up" moment is a moment of mindfulness, pulling you out of your trance and into the present moment.

For your informal mindfulness practice, pick an activity you do every day (like taking a shower, washing the dishes, making the bed, or going for a walk) and see what it's like to pay full attention to what is happening right here and now. In the shower, do you feel the water on your body? Is it warm enough? Is it too hot? Do you feel the soap or the shampoo? Can you be present throughout the shower? If your mind wanders, bring it back to the sensory experience of being in the shower.

This week, try to schedule at least three or four formal sitting meditation sessions and one or two informal practices. During each activity, practice being mindful: Notice how your body feels, notice your breath, and notice any sensory experiences, such as what you see, hear, smell, or touch. Write down your experiences and your responses.

Date	Practice	Response

What did you find challenging about this exercise?

_____

_____

_____

Describe how you felt after practicing mindful meditation for one week. Did you find that your stress and/or anxiety was reduced?

_____

_____

_____

worksheet

Become Mindful of Your World Rather Than Your Anxious Thoughts

Objective

To focus on the world using your five senses rather than on your anxious thoughts.

What to Know

Do you often find yourself agonizing over what might happen in the future, worrying about every possible thing that might go wrong, while simultaneously condemning yourself for what went wrong in the past? Being consumed by all this turmoil does not allow you to appreciate or enjoy what you are experiencing in the present moment, such as a birthday celebration or even a simple night out with your friends.

Anxiety disorders can demand that you ignore what's taking place around you by bombarding you with disturbing thoughts, urges, and images. These unwanted experiences distract you from living your life in the moment and instead encourage you to obsess about a past you cannot change and an uncertain future you cannot predict or control.

What if you tried to live your life according to the uplifting and freeing principles of mindfulness instead of the rigid rules of your anxiety disorder? Mindfulness encourages you to notice and accept your thoughts, while at the same time not allowing you to be obsessed with them. By teaching you to focus on the present moment in a meaningful, nonjudgmental way, it takes away the power of your anxious thoughts.

What to Do

This exercise will encourage you to draw your attention away from your anxious thoughts and toward yourself, using your five senses as a guide.

- Commit to using your sight, hearing, touch, taste, and smell to channel your thoughts in a purposeful direction.
- Commit to doing this at least once a day for at least three weeks until you become accustomed to focusing your mind on the present.
- Begin by focusing on one sense for at least one to two minutes, taking the time to truly separate that sense from the next as you move from one to the other.

It does not matter what order you practice the five senses in. You can switch them around as you see fit. You can sit in a comfortable position the first few times, and as you become accustomed to performing the exercise, you can engage in it at any time or place.

At first this exercise may seem silly to you, and even somewhat difficult, but as you continue to practice you will find it easier to incorporate mindfulness into your daily experience until it becomes a natural part of who you are.

Five Senses Mindfulness Exercise

Sight

- Observe what is around you, noticing its shape, color, and texture.
- Look for things you would not usually take the time to notice, such as shadows, a crack in the sidewalk, the texture of your bedspread, or any other small details that usually escape you.

Sound

- Take the time to listen to what is in the background instead of what is obvious. For example:
  - Don't just notice the sound of laughter, but try to discern different types of laughs.
  - Rather than simply listening for the sounds of traffic, try to distinguish horns honking from tires squealing.
  - Instead of bristling at loud music, take the time to figure out what genre you are hearing.
  - Listen to previously unnoticed sounds, like the hum of the refrigerator or the clicking of the oven as it cycles on and off.

Touch

- Become aware of the differing feel of everyday items that surround you.
- Alternate touching items that are cold and warm, and notice how they make your hands feel.
- Touch items with various textures to notice the difference among them.
- Play with modeling clay or pet an animal, and notice the sensations in your fingers and hands as you feel your motions unfolding.

Taste

- Take a drink, and notice the feeling of the liquid rolling over your tongue.
- Chew on a piece of gum or candy, and take the time to notice the taste from when you first put it in your mouth until you finish it.

Smell

- Focus your attention on your surroundings to notice what different smells are in the air.
- Keep strong-smelling gum or candy with you to quietly smell in order to center yourself when you feel your anxiety rising. Other items such as lavender, perfume, or lotion also can provide a satisfying aroma that invokes mindfulness.

Five Senses Meditation Chart

For a five-day period, set aside at least 20 minutes per day to practice this meditation, focusing on a different sense each day. For each sense, choose one suggestion from the mindfulness exercise to focus on.

	Sense	Focus of Your Meditation	What Did You Notice?	What Feelings Came Up?
Day 1				
Day 2				
Day 3				
Day 4				
Day 5				

After practicing mindfulness, what did you notice that you had not previously noticed?

_____

_____

_____

Over time, how did practicing mindfulness impact your ability to focus on the present?

_____

_____

_____

What difficulties did you encounter in practicing your mindfulness exercises? What changes did you make, if any, to make it easier for you?

_____

_____

_____

How can you integrate the practice of mindfulness into your life to help you manage your anxiety?

_____

_____

_____

Change Your Thinking

section 4

Own Your Thoughts

Objective

To decrease the power your thoughts have over you by learning to separate your interpretation of your thoughts from the thoughts themselves.

What to Know

Have you ever imagined yourself engaging in some unthinkable, inappropriate behavior, such as standing up and screaming in a classroom where everyone is silent or walking by a fire alarm and pulling it? This is completely normal. Everyone has thoughts that are weird, unpleasant, and even disturbing at times. Most teens will quickly have the disturbing thought and then just as quickly forget about it.

You might define these types of thoughts as "good" or "bad" and then judge yourself as being good or bad based on the thoughts you have. You might even be tempted to fight against the thought by controlling it or trying to stop it altogether.

If you have obsessive thoughts, you might have a different experience in which you not only can't let the upsetting thought go but also find yourself attaching personal meaning to it, elevating it to the point where your obsession becomes entrenched. Trying to control a thought or stop it are strategies that do not help stop obsessions and most likely make them stronger.

Instead, learn to regard the thoughts clinically, as facts that can be explored to determine their worth in shaping your life. Practice categorizing your thoughts, not as good or bad, but as limiting or expanding your life, encouraging or discouraging you to thrive, or simply being helpful or unhelpful to you.

What to Do

Answer the following questions about each obsessive thought you have. You can use additional paper, if needed.

What am I obsessing about?

_____

_____

_____

What does this thought mean? How does this thought make me feel about myself?

_____

_____

_____

How likely is it this thought will come true?

_____

_____

_____

Use a simple two-minute meditation:

- Close your eyes.
- Breathe deeply in and out.
- Imagine a group of gnats buzzing around you. As they circle your head, realize they are annoying but harmless—you can deal with them.
- Now picture your disturbing thoughts as if they are noisy bugs flying at a distance. You can hear them, but they are in the background. Imagine ignoring them, focusing on something else.
- Even though it might feel uncomfortable, add some uncertainty to your usual response to your obsessive thought by asking yourself, "What might happen if I didn't do anything about this?"
- Allow at least five minutes to go by before you take any action.
- Extend the time by an additional five minutes every time you have the thought, until you don't feel the need to respond at all.

Become Aware of the Physical Reactions to Your Distressing Thoughts

Objective

To practice mindfulness to reduce physical reactions to distressing thoughts.

What to Know

When you have anxiety, just thinking about something can upset you and cause your body to react. Your thoughts can trigger a physical response in your body, like tightness in your chest or digestive upset, leading to increased anxiety. Sometimes, this can result in a panic attack. Major distress can start with just a simple thought.

Mindfulness increases your awareness of the present moment. You can acknowledge your thoughts without reacting in a judgmental or negative way. Being nonjudgmental is the key, and that's what we're going to work on with this exercise, as it's designed to help you become aware of upsetting thoughts *without* triggering a physical response in your body.

What to Do

Get comfortable and read the following unpleasant phrases. Choose one to focus on. For at least five minutes, visualize the image using all the appropriate senses: sight, sound, smell, touch, and taste. Even though the images are very unpleasant, don't judge them. See if you can be mindful and present without negative physical reactions.

1. A person vomiting on you
2. Opening a door and finding a dead animal in the room
3. Looking at an open, oozing sore
4. Sitting in a dark cave with insects crawling around you
5. Drowning or suffocating

Think of other disgusting or upsetting images:

6. _____
7. _____

Practice this mindfulness technique with two of the preceding repellant phrases for five minutes each. Rate how you did with each, using a scale of 1 to 10, where 1 is "I didn't respond to the image at all" and 10 is "I was completely disgusted by the visualization and felt really uncomfortable."

Situation: _____

Experience: _____

Rating: _____

Situation: _____

Experience: _____

Rating: _____

Now, describe one situation that normally causes you to be very anxious and upset.

_____

_____

_____

Using the chart on the following page, mindfully and nonjudgmentally think about this anxiety-provoking situation for at least five minutes each day. Do this at least once a day for seven days.

Date and Time	Describe How You Felt	Rating (1–10)

After you have practiced this exercise for one week, describe any changes in your physical reactions.

_____

_____

_____

What did you find challenging about this exercise?

_____

_____

_____

Did you find that your anxiety was reduced after doing this exercise for one week?

_____

_____

_____

Confront Thoughts That Make You Anxious

Objective

To address and accept rather than avoid thoughts that make you anxious.

What to Know

Avoiding your worries just makes them worse. You might seek ways to distract yourself from thoughts that make you anxious; unfortunately, this is the opposite of what you should be doing. The more you simply accept and allow your thoughts to happen—even the most disturbing ones—the less power they will have over you.

In this worksheet, you will practice confronting thoughts that make you anxious rather than avoiding them.

What to Do

The following activity will force you to have anxiety-provoking thoughts over and over again until they lose their power over you. As you do this activity, remember: *These are thoughts, and thinking them cannot make bad things happen.*

Begin by writing down an upsetting thought that you normally try to avoid because it makes you anxious.

_____

_____

_____

What do you usually do to avoid upsetting thoughts that make you anxious?

_____

_____

_____

Now choose one or two of the following activities that will force you to have this thought:

_____ Write down this thought at least 25 times on a sheet of paper.

_____ Sing this thought to the tune of "Happy Birthday" (or another tune).

_____ Draw a picture of the worst thing this thought represents.

_____ Say this thought in front of a mirror for three minutes.

_____ Make a recording of this thought and play it for at least five minutes.

_____ Create a collage representing this thought, cutting out words from newspapers or magazines and pasting in pictures that represent what the thought is about.

_____ Say the thought at least ten times in a ridiculous voice.

_____ Translate the thought into another language and repeat it in that language several times.

Keep track of how you're feeling when you try the activities. Do at least one activity every day for at least one week. Rate how upsetting you found this thought after each activity on a scale of 1 to 10, where 1 is "not really upsetting" and 10 is "the worst anxiety you've experienced."

Date	Activity	Length of Time	Rating

Which activity did you find most helpful in confronting your thoughts, and why?

_____

_____

_____

What did you find most challenging about this activity?

_____

_____

_____

Do you still feel that you have to avoid thoughts that make you anxious? If the answer is "yes," continue this exercise for another week. Then, describe your experience.

_____

_____

_____

Five Steps to Deal with Intrusive Thoughts

Objective

To cope with intrusive and recurring thoughts by accepting them rather than fighting them.

What to Know

Everyone has unacceptable intrusive thoughts sometimes. Take a look at these examples:

- Josh walked down the corridor of his school and suddenly had the thought that he might pull the fire alarm.
- Samantha stood near the edge of the rooftop of her building and suddenly thought she might jump off.
- Nadia was sitting in church and she suddenly felt like she might shout out some obscene words.

Most of the time, these are passing thoughts. Although they might be totally unacceptable and completely out of character, they come and go very quickly, and minutes later you forget all about them. In many ways, they are more of a curiosity than a problem.

But, for some teens, intrusive and unacceptable thoughts get "stuck" in their brains. For example, a common intrusive thought among people with anxiety is that something will happen to a family member, and they will be hurt or even killed.

Unfortunately, the more you try to get rid of intrusive thoughts, the more they are sure to come back. Instead of trying to fight your intrusive thoughts, accept them. This worksheet can help you do just that.

What to Do

You will be using these five steps to learn to accept your intrusive thoughts:

1. Label your intrusive thoughts as "just thoughts." Remind yourself that they have no power over you.
2. Tell yourself that these thoughts are just your brain going on "automatic," and you can safely ignore them.
3. Accept and allow the thoughts into your mind. Don't try to push them away.

4. Breathe from your diaphragm until your anxiety starts to decrease.

5. Continue whatever you were doing prior to the intrusive thought.

This may seem strange, but the next thing you need to do is to *practice* having upsetting thoughts. Forcing yourself to have the upsetting thoughts you have been avoiding is the only way you can learn to accept them with the five-step procedure. When you learn to accept your upsetting intrusive thoughts rather than fighting them, they will soon stop being a big part of your life.

Using the chart on the following page, each day write down *all* of the triggers and intrusive thoughts that you regularly have (even if you didn't have that particular thought on that particular day. Then, rate the distress you experience while having these thoughts on a scale of 1 to 10, where 1 is "they really don't bother me" and 10 is "I can't stand them anymore." Practice the five-step acceptance procedure (this will normally take 15 to 20 minutes). Finally, rate your distress again. Do this every day for at least two weeks, and see if your intrusive thoughts are still playing a big part in your life. You might need to make copies of this chart.

Date and Time	Trigger Situations	Intrusive Thoughts	Level of Distress Before (1–10)	Level of Distress After (1–10)

Did this practice decrease the intensity of your intrusive thoughts? How so?

_____

_____

_____

Your Mind Is Playing Tricks on You

Objective

To understand that your worries are not real and that your mind is just playing tricks on you.

What to Know

Do you watch scary movies? Do you cover your eyes when you see gore? Do you jump or even scream when some horrible monster suddenly appears with sharp teeth or a knife in its hand? Part of the fun of watching these movies is the powerful emotional and visceral reactions you have because your mind is tricking you into thinking that what you are watching is real, even though you know you are just sitting watching a movie in the theater or at home.

This is a little like what happens when you let your worries control your mind. It's like you are watching a "worry movie" in your head, expecting something bad to happen, and you feel like it's real. This movie in your head might even cause physical reactions in your body: Your heart might speed up, you might feel sweaty, or your stomach might feel like it is tied in a knot.

The difference, of course, is that when you leave the movie theater or turn off the TV, you are fully aware that your reaction was a fantasy. You might think about the special effects in the movie, the actors, or the way other people reacted. You might be thinking about doing your homework or going out with friends. You're back to reality.

However, when you play a movie that features the worries in your head, you never really leave the theater or turn off the TV. You might say to yourself, "This probably won't happen" or "I'm stupid for thinking about this," but your mind and your body never quite accept the fact that your worries aren't based in reality and the things you're imagining aren't really dangerous.

What to Do

Begin by drawing a picture of your most disturbing worry as if it were a movie playing on a screen. Include as many details as you can in the picture, and give the movie a title. Then, complete the steps that follow to observe your worries without responding to them as if they were real.

Title: _____

Activities to Teach Your Mind Your Worries Are Not Real

Find a really scary movie to watch at home. Before you turn it on, relax in a comfortable chair and breathe deeply for about five minutes. Now, remind yourself this is just a movie. Skip to a place in the movie that you know will be scary, but emotionally distance yourself from what is going on so that you don't react with fear. Pretend that you are watching an ordinary event, like a garbage truck picking up the trash.

How successful were you at blocking your emotional reaction to the scary movie? Rate yourself on a scale of 1 to 10, where 1 is "not at all successful" and 10 is "very successful." _____

Describe how easy or difficult this was for you.

_____

_____

_____

_____

Now sit back, relax, and close your eyes. Pretend that you're watching a movie of your worries. Think about whatever worries you most, making the images in your mind as real as possible. Include all the details as if you were watching an actual movie. Again, emotionally distance yourself from what is going on in your worry movie. Pretend that it's just a documentary about something vaguely interesting to you.

How successful were you at blocking your emotional reaction? Rate yourself on a scale of 1 to 10, where 1 is "not at all successful" and 10 is "very successful." _____

Describe how easy or difficult this was for you.

_____

_____

_____

_____

Run your worry movie in your head for five to ten minutes every night for one week. Use the following chart to record how successful you were at thinking about your worries but not reacting to them emotionally. Rate yourself on a scale of 1 to 10, where 1 is "not at all successful" and 10 is "very successful."

Date	Rating	Reflect on How You Felt

Did this exercise change the way you perceive your worries? How so? Were you successful in decreasing your emotional response to your worries? Explain.

_____

_____

_____

worksheet

You Don't Need Constant Reassurance

Objective

To reduce your need for reassurance.

What to Know

You might be surprised to learn that an excessive need for reassurance is considered to be a compulsion. It's a compulsion because it's an act carried out repeatedly with the expectation of relieving anxiety.

Excessive reassurance-seeking is sometimes compared to an addictive behavior because you can never engage in this compulsive act just once, kind of like eating potato chips. You can never eat just one, and instead you find yourself compelled by some mysterious force to eat one after another until every chip is gone.

What to Do

1. Give yourself permission to seek reassurance, and keep track of the average amount of time you spend engaging in it.
2. Make a plan to delay seeking reassurance for at least 15 minutes after you notice the signs that your obsessive thoughts are triggering you.
3. Practice delaying seeking reassurance for two weeks.
4. At the end of two weeks, increase the time you delay seeking reassurance for an additional 15 minutes.
5. Continue to repeat this exercise until you no longer need to seek reassurance.

Write down your worry:

_____

Write down your goal:

_____

_____

_____

How long will you delay seeking reassurance? _____

Ask yourself these questions before you seek reassurance:

- Does what I am doing help or hinder my enjoyment of life?
- Does what I am doing match what I value in my life?
- Does what I am doing make me feel happy or upset?
- Does what I am doing propel my emotional, social, psychological, or academic goals or stop them in their tracks?

Complete the following chart for two weeks (you may need to make multiple copies). Describe the worry and rate your anxiety before and after you seek reassurance on a scale of 1 to 10, where 1 is "no anxiety" and 10 is "severe anxiety." Include whether or not you were able to delay seeking reassurance and the amount of time you delayed seeking reassurance.

Date	Worry That Prompted You to Seek Reassurance	Anxiety Level (1–10)	Delay Time	Did You Successfully Delay Seeking Reassurance? (Yes or No)	Anxiety Level (1–10)
Example: *March 15*	*I am worried that I will catch the flu from my sister.*	*9*	*30 minutes*	*Yes, I was able to wait 30 minutes before I asked my mom if she thinks I'll catch the flu.*	*6*

Did you delay seeking reassurance most of the time? Some of the time? Not at all?

_____

_____

_____

What would it take to make delaying reassurance easier for you?

_____

_____

_____

What strategies did you use to delay seeking reassurance?

_____

_____

_____

worksheet

Tolerate and Overcome Physical Discomfort

Objective

To replicate uncomfortable physical sensations associated with anxiety in order to tolerate and overcome those sensations.

What to Know

You might experience physical discomfort when you are fearful and anxious. If you think about a class presentation you have to deliver, your heart might beat faster, your chest may tighten, you may sweat, and you may even feel like you are going to faint.

These physical reactions can be scary, and you might feel like you are having a heart attack or like you are disconnected from reality. When this happens, you can become just as afraid of the physical reactions as you are of the actual situation that causes your anxiety.

There is one way to break this cycle of anxiety and fear: Practice the physical sensations that make you nervous and panicky. If this doesn't sound like fun, you're right—it isn't. But pushing through and completing this exercise will help you reduce the discomfort and anxiety you feel going forward, making your efforts worthwhile!

What to Do

First, identify the physical sensations that accompany your anxiety. In the following chart, circle the physical symptoms you have when you are anxious. If there are other symptoms you have that are missing from the chart, add them at the end.

Next, you will *intentionally* create those uncomfortable feelings. The second column of the chart gives you some ideas of how to do this. Practice these methods several times with a "spotter" in the room, such as a friend or family member. This person will encourage you to perform the exercises so that you mimic the physical sensations associated with your anxiety, and they will also protect you from any possible physical injury, like falling if you get dizzy.

Uncomfortable Feelings	How to Create Those Feelings
Lightheadedness	Hyperventilate for one minute. Breathe loudly and rapidly (similar to a panting dog) at a rate of approximately 45 breaths per minute.
Feeling faint	Place your head between your legs for one minute, then quickly sit up.
Feelings of unreality	Think of how big the universe is and how small you are.
	Think about the 200,000 years that humans have been on the earth and all of your ancestors.
	Sit in a completely dark and completely quiet room for five minutes.
Blurred vision	Stare at a lightbulb for one minute and then attempt to read.
Difficulty breathing	Hold your nose and breathe through a thin straw for one minute.
Increased heart rate	Drink an espresso or other caffeinated drink.
Tightness in your chest	Do five minutes of moderately intensive cardiovascular exercise, like running up and down the stairs.
Upset stomach	Do 20 jumping jacks after a meal.
Feeling shaky	Tense all of your muscles and hold the tension for one minute.
Sweating	Wear a jacket or wrap yourself in a blanket in a hot room.
Feeling dizzy	Spin around really fast for one minute.
Other physical symptoms:	How can you replicate these feelings?

The phrase "practice makes perfect" has never been truer than for people overcoming and tolerating physical discomfort. Although it's unpleasant, practicing the uncomfortable feelings will help you master your anxiety, change your thinking, and decrease your worry about physical symptoms. For two weeks, practice inducing these physical sensations once per day. Rate your anxiety about each session on a scale of 1 to 10, where 1 is "no anxiety" and 10 is "extreme anxiety."

Date and Time	Physical Sensations	Emotional Reaction	Thoughts	Rating (1–10)

After practicing the physical sensations that make you nervous and panicky for two weeks, how did your body sensations, feelings, and thoughts change?

_____

_____

_____

How was your anxiety affected? Did it increase, decrease, or stay the same?

_____

_____

_____

worksheet

Anticipate Success

Objective

To visualize yourself solving a current problem so you increase your chances of success and reduce your anxiety.

What to Know

Sometimes you unconsciously create your future. Without thinking about it, you put yourself in situations or make decisions based on needs or conflicts of which you're not really aware. You might unintentionally make things worse for yourself or others. However, your mind can also work to make your life better.

Recognizing the importance of your unconscious wishes and needs, solution-oriented therapy asks you to concentrate on how things will be in a future where your problems have less influence or may be absent altogether.

This worksheet will help you focus on the positive aspects of your life rather than on the problems. Sometimes your unconscious needs direct your decision-making and lead to anxiety. Instead, you can learn to solve problems in a productive and beneficial way, reducing your stress and anxiety. The concept of a self-fulfilling prophecy is a very real psychological phenomenon. You can make your future better or worse. Why not make it better?

What to Do

Describe a problem you have.

_____

_____

_____

Imagine this problem is gone in one year. Describe how your life has changed.

_____

_____

_____

_____

Now reread what you wrote in the previous question. Does anything come to mind that will make this happen? Even if it isn't directly related to the problem, write it down.

_____

_____

_____

_____

What changes can you make now to move you toward your future? Be specific.

_____

_____

_____

_____

Reread your answers frequently, perhaps once a week. Keep thinking about the future you described. Convince yourself that it can happen. Keep thinking about even the simplest ways to make positive changes in your life.

worksheet

Fill Your Mind with Positive Thoughts

Objective

To increase positive thinking to reduce anxiety and bring a greater sense of well-being.

What to Know

If you're anxious, it's important to accept these thoughts rather than fight them or avoid them. In other words, you can tolerate anxious thoughts and understand that they are just thoughts and cannot hurt you.

Here is a four-step procedure to help you deal with these distressing thoughts:

1. Recognize and label your thoughts.
2. Observe them rather than react to them.
3. Replace anxious thoughts with positive affirmations or thoughts.
4. Allow time to pass.

Paying attention to positive thoughts may have many benefits, and continued practice can even help rewire your brain. Replacing anxious thoughts with positive thinking can help you better cope with stress, reduce your anxiety, and even improve your health.

This worksheet is designed to help you focus on positive thoughts to reduce your anxiety and improve your overall sense of well-being. You will write down positive thoughts in a journal for two weeks and then reflect on whether this activity helps you focus less on your anxious thoughts.

What to Do

Get a journal or notebook, and each day pick an activity from the following list. Use one page for each activity. Complete at least one activity a day for two weeks. At the end of the two weeks, answer the questions about how this activity helped you and how it impacted your anxiety.

Activity	Date Completed
Write down five of your best qualities.	
Describe a favorite memory.	
Describe in detail the best day of your life.	
Make a list of your five most precious possessions.	
Make a "bucket list" of five things you'd like to do.	
Write down five positive adjectives to describe yourself.	
Write down a list of five favorite people you have known in your life.	
Write down five things you'd like to do with your family.	
Write down five things you'd like to do with your friends.	
Write down five people who inspire you.	
Write down five things for which you're grateful.	
Write about a dream place you would like to live.	
Write about a favorite sports hero and why you admire them.	
Describe something that makes you proud.	
Describe a memorable birthday.	
Describe a favorite holiday and what you like about it.	
Describe a favorite place in nature.	
Write down a favorite dream you can remember.	
Write down a favorite memory from your early childhood.	
Write down five things you are good at.	
Find and write down three inspirational quotes.	
Describe what you would do if you won $10 million.	
Write down the names of five people you love.	
Write down five people that have positively influenced you.	
Write down five things you have accomplished.	
Write down five good things that happened at school.	
Write down three vacations you would like to take.	
Write down a list of the five funniest movies or TV shows you enjoy.	
Describe a favorite character from a book.	
Describe a favorite character from a movie.	
Write down any positive thoughts you're having today.	

At the end of the two weeks, answer the following questions.

Did you notice any change in your thoughts over the last two weeks? When did this happen? Describe your experience.

_____

_____

_____

Ask people who know you well whether they noticed anything different about you in the last two weeks. Write down what they said.

_____

_____

_____

Describe any changes you noticed in your anxiety over the last two weeks. Did it decrease?

_____

_____

_____

What was your favorite assignment out of all of the activities you completed, and why?

_____

_____

_____

Lifestyle Changes

section 5

Changing Your Diet to Help Your Anxiety

Objective

To improve your diet to decrease anxiety symptoms.

What to Know

If you have anxiety, you might feel physically unwell. Watching what you eat may help. Since diet, stress, and mood are all intertwined, it's important to consider what you're consuming—not only for your physical health, but also for your emotional well-being. It's not necessary to go to extremes in changing your diet. By simply being more mindful of what you eat, you can find small ways to improve how you feel.

You might want to *avoid* these items to reduce anxiety:

- **Caffeine.** This stimulant is in coffee, tea, chocolate, soda, energy drinks, and some over-the-counter medications. The temporary boost it provides can end in fatigue, headache, and tension. Caffeine is a potential trigger for anxiety attacks and a contributor to other health issues, such as insomnia, heartburn, aggression, irritability, heart palpitations, and high blood pressure.
- **Salt.** Sodium is present in many processed foods, so check labels and look for low-sodium or salt-free alternatives. Sodium consumption affects fluid retention, weight, and blood pressure, all of which, in turn, can affect your mood.
- **Sugar.** Excessive intake of simple sugars (such as white or brown sugar and honey) can cause health problems, such as diabetes and hypoglycemia—the latter of which is often accompanied by symptoms similar to those experienced during a panic attack. Also, the temporary uplifting effects come with some other serious downsides, including an increased risk of depression in those who have a sugar-heavy diet.
- **Preservatives and hormones.** These substances are present in processed foods and many types of meats. Our bodies were not built to handle these additives, and their possible side effects have been heavily debated. Swapping in some whole, unprocessed, organic foods can help reduce consumption of these potentially harmful substances.
- **Nicotine and alcohol.** Introducing these substances into your system can cause a range of problems, including aggravating anxiety. Nicotine is a stimulant, like caffeine, and alcohol a depressant. Both can affect your sleep.

What can you eat to improve symptoms of anxiety? Try the following suggestions.

- **Eat a protein-rich breakfast.** You'll feel fuller longer and your blood sugar will remain steady so that you have more energy. Some protein-rich options are eggs, lean meats, cottage cheese, Greek yogurt, tofu, and nuts.
- **Eat complex carbohydrates.** Carbohydrates increase the amount of serotonin in your brain, which is calming. Eat foods rich in complex carbohydrates, such as oatmeal, quinoa, whole-grain breads or cereals, beans, and peas.
- **Drink plenty of water.** Even mild dehydration can affect your mood.
- **Pay attention to food sensitivities.** Some foods or food additives can cause unpleasant physical reactions, which may lead to irritability or anxiety.
- **Regularly eat healthy, balanced meals.** Nutritious foods are important for overall physical and mental health. Eat lots of fresh fruits and vegetables. It may also help to eat foods high in omega-3 fatty acids, such as salmon and walnuts, on a regular basis. Nutrient deficiencies can cause irritability, anxiety, and fatigue.

Changes to your diet will make some difference to your general mood and well-being, but it's not necessarily a substitute for treatment. Other lifestyle changes—such as improving your sleep habits, increasing your social support, using stress-reduction techniques, and getting regular exercise—will also help.

What to Do

For the next month, keep track of what you eat and drink, and describe how you feel each day. Rate your anxiety symptoms on a scale of 1 to 10, where 1 is "little or no anxiety" and 10 is "severe anxiety." You can make copies of the following chart or use a notebook or journal.

Week of: _____

Day	Food and Beverages Consumed	Substances or Medications	Anxiety Symptoms	Anxiety Level (1–10)
Monday				
Tuesday				
Wednesday				
Thursday				
Friday				
Saturday				
Sunday				

After tracking your food and beverage consumption for one month, describe your experiences. Include how your anxiety symptoms changed.

_____

_____

_____

_____

What did you add or exclude? Did it make a difference? Did it increase or decrease your anxiety symptoms?

_____

_____

_____

_____

What other changes can you make?

_____

_____

_____

_____

Mindfulness—Just This Breath

Objective

To focus on the present to increase feelings of calm and well-being.

What to Know

This 7-minute mindfulness audio file is designed to help anxious teens by providing them an opportunity focus on the present. The audio is courtesy of Dartmouth College Health Services, with a script made at Georgia Southern University Counseling Center and editing by Martin Grant. You can access the file here: https://www.betweensessions.com/wp-content/uploads/2021/10/BS_Calming_Your_Body_1-1.mp3

You can download this file to your preferred device and use it whenever you are feeling anxious or stressed.

Use the following chart to record your daily relaxation practice. Make several copies of this chart, and keep a record of the time you spend practicing this relaxation technique until it is truly a habit. You want it to become routine—something you do without thinking, like brushing your teeth. It is also useful to note your general mood, both before and after your daily relaxation exercise.

Date	Time of Day	Minutes	Mood Before Relaxation	Mood After Relaxation

worksheet

Stretch Out of Your Comfort Zone

Objective

To take steps toward new and different life experiences by identifying your comfort zone and thinking about how you can move beyond it.

What to Know

The idea of going out of your comfort zone might feel scary. If you feel anxious in social situations, tend to isolate, are shy, or otherwise avoid people or unfamiliar situations, it can be especially challenging.

Changing habits is hard. You might have resistance to—and fear of—change. You have a comfort zone: the things, objects, people, activities, and habits that keep you feeling safe. But here's the catch. Changing habits in a big way inevitably involves some discomfort.

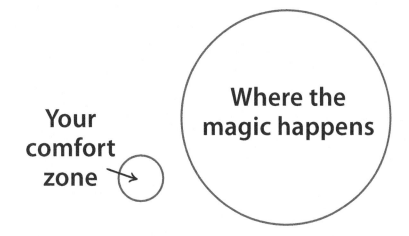

Isn't this a great image? First, the magic circle is a lot bigger than the comfort zone circle. That's encouraging! But see that empty space between the circles? That space represents the unknown, which can be both exciting and scary.

To get from one circle to the other, you'll have to navigate some unknown territory. Have you ever heard the saying "Leap and the net will appear"? It's the same idea. With good planning and good support, you can succeed. But there are no guarantees. As Yoda from the *Star Wars* movies said, "Do or do not. There is no try."

What to Do

In this exercise, you'll identify the components of your personal comfort zone. Next, you'll imagine "where the magic happens" for you. Then, you'll identify some concrete steps to take to guide you along your journey.

What are the components of your comfort zone? What helps you feel safe but might be interfering with moving forward? Be as detailed as you can.

Things/Objects

_____

_____

_____

_____

People

_____

_____

_____

_____

Activities

_____

_____

_____

_____

Habits

_____

_____

_____

_____

What are your thoughts and feelings about the unknown (that blank space between the circles)? What has helped in the past when you succeeded in moving out of your comfort zone and into the unknown in your life? List the items that helped you.

_____

_____

_____

_____

_____

What items in your list represent "where the magic happens" for you?

_____

_____

_____

_____

_____

What steps are you willing to take to get closer to "where the magic happens" for you? Be detailed. Be optimistic while still being realistic.

Today

_____

_____

_____

Tomorrow

_____

_____

_____

In the next week

_____

_____

_____

In the next month

_____

_____

_____

In the next year

_____

_____

_____

Exercise to Overcome Anxiety

Objective

To exercise consistently to reduce your anxiety.

What to Know

Regular exercise can help you overcome your anxiety. During exercise, your brain increases the production of chemicals that can lift your mood and regulate your emotions. With regular exercise, you'll feel stronger, more confident, and better able to make positive changes in your life. Exercise will also increase the oxygen flow to your brain, which may help you think more clearly, rationally, and positively.

1. Circle the types of exercise you could do on a regular basis.

Bike riding	Baseball	Football	Handball
Jogging	Hiking	Soccer	Karate or other martial arts
Walking	Skateboarding	Surfing	Pilates
Weightlifting	Basketball	Skiing	Yoga
Tennis	Swimming	Dancing	Golf

   Write down other physical activities you could do that aren't listed.

   _____

   _____

   _____

2. Now, choose three exercises you would like to do over the next week.

   a. _____

   b. _____

   c. _____

3. How much time you need for each exercise? How often can you do each activity?

a. _____

b. _____

c. _____

Use this chart to record how many times you actually exercise and the effect that exercise has on your anxiety.

Day	Type of Exercise	Amount of Time	Mood Before	Mood After
Monday				
Tuesday				
Wednesday				
Thursday				
Friday				
Saturday				
Sunday				

After one week of consistent exercise, did you feel less anxious, more anxious, or about the same? _____

What was your favorite form of exercise, and why? Can you continue practicing this activity?

_____

_____

_____

worksheet

Sleeping Better to Reduce Anxiety

Objective

To track your sleep and the methods you use to sleep better in order to decrease anxiety symptoms.

What to Know

Do you have a hard time falling asleep or staying asleep? Anxiety causes sleep problems, and research indicates lack of sleep can aggravate anxiety. Sleep deprivation may actually play a key role in stimulating brain regions that contribute to excessive worrying and adversely alter serotonin levels, which can affect your mood. There are a variety of techniques that can help you get the sleep you need, but, of course, they only work if you are diligent at trying them and then use the ones that work best. Getting enough sleep is an important part of your overall plan to overcome your anxiety—and it's also important for your general health.

Here are some things you can try for better sleep:

- Listen to soft music, read, take a warm shower, or meditate before going to bed.
- Exercise for at least 30 minutes each day, but not immediately before you go to bed.
- Write a to-do list for the following day, and then clear your head of those concerns.
- Practice deep breathing or progressive muscle relaxation before you fall asleep.
- Avoid caffeine, alcohol, and nicotine, either entirely or at least in the evening.
- Keep your bedroom at a cool temperature (60–65 degrees).
- If you are sensitive to light, try wearing a sleep mask. If you are sensitive to sound, try wearing earplugs or using a white-noise machine. There are also various white-noise apps available.
- If you have trouble falling asleep, get out of bed and do some light activity (like reading) in another room. Go back to bed when you feel drowsy.
- Go to bed and get up at the same time every day.
- Avoid eating heavy meals for at least two to three hours before bed.
- Make sure your mattress and pillows are comfortable.

What to Do

For two weeks, use the following chart to track your sleep and the methods you use to sleep better.

Date	Hours Slept	Trouble Sleeping?		Methods Tried	Successful?	
		☐ Yes	☐ No		☐ Yes	☐ No
		☐ Yes	☐ No		☐ Yes	☐ No
		☐ Yes	☐ No		☐ Yes	☐ No
		☐ Yes	☐ No		☐ Yes	☐ No
		☐ Yes	☐ No		☐ Yes	☐ No
		☐ Yes	☐ No		☐ Yes	☐ No
		☐ Yes	☐ No		☐ Yes	☐ No
		☐ Yes	☐ No		☐ Yes	☐ No
		☐ Yes	☐ No		☐ Yes	☐ No
		☐ Yes	☐ No		☐ Yes	☐ No
		☐ Yes	☐ No		☐ Yes	☐ No
		☐ Yes	☐ No		☐ Yes	☐ No
		☐ Yes	☐ No		☐ Yes	☐ No
		☐ Yes	☐ No		☐ Yes	☐ No

What two activities helped you the most?

1. _____

2. _____

Was it hard to fall asleep and stay asleep? If so, why?

_____

_____

_____

Prevent and Manage Lapses in Overcoming Your Anxiety

Objective

To increase your awareness of when you are at risk for a lapse by identifying early warning signs and planning how to respond.

What to Know

As you start to successfully manage your anxiety, you'll see that your symptoms will begin to decrease or even disappear. However, you should know that at some point there may be a temporary reappearance of symptoms. This is called a *lapse*, and it's common. The more prepared you are for a lapse to happen in the future, the more likely it is that you will successfully get through it.

Lapses can occur while you are still in counseling or months after you have finished treatment. Lapses tend to happen during times of high stress, when you allow yourself to loosen up on using your coping skills or start to make unhealthy choices.

This worksheet will help you develop a plan to respond to a lapse now so that you know what to do if and when it happens. When you manage your lapses, you are actively decreasing the risk that a relapse will occur.

What to Do

Here are some tips that can help you prevent or manage a lapse:

- Remember that lapses are normal because stress happens.
- Lapses can be clues to stressful situations that require change.
- Be patient. Remember that change takes time, and a lapse does not mean you are back at square one.
- Don't avoid your anxiety. Be honest with yourself about your symptoms and what you are doing to cope.
- Reach out to someone if you need help. You don't have to suffer through anxiety alone.
- If you see symptoms creeping up, don't give up on yourself! A lapse can be discouraging, but you always have a choice to work through it.

- Don't mask your anxiety. Be careful of behaviors that temporarily give you comfort but limit your ability to make healthy choices, such as drinking alcohol.
- Live a balanced life. Managing anxiety is not just about coping skills. A healthy diet, restful sleep, exercise, hobbies, and fun activities all contribute to a balanced life.
- If you have been prescribed medication for your anxiety, keep taking it as prescribed. Talk to your parents or caregivers if you're thinking about stopping.

What are the people, places, thoughts, behaviors, or things that trigger your anxiety? In other words, what makes you anxious?

_____

_____

_____

_____

Identify your warning signs for a lapse by writing down the main symptoms you felt when you first began counseling. Try to be as specific as possible because the longer you live without the symptoms of anxiety, the more difficult it may be to look back and remember how much anxiety once impacted your life.

_____

_____

_____

_____

Make a plan to prevent or manage lapses by writing down the two coping skills that you've found most helpful in decreasing your anxiety. Include details about why these skills have helped you or why you like using them. You'll want to revisit these coping skills if a lapse comes up.

1. _____

How does this help you?

_____

_____

_____

_____

2. _____

How does this help you?

_____

_____

_____

_____

For your convenience, purchasers can download and print
the worksheets from www.pesi.com/AnxiousTeens

67785421R00109